Service Above Self

A History of the Bowling Green Rotary Club
and the City That Made it All Possible

Larry J. Pack

The Bowling Green Rotary Club
2010

Committee to Publish the
History of the Bowling Green Rotary Club

Charles M. Moore, Jr., Chairman
Carroll Hildreth
Charles Hardcastle
Bob Hovious
Bill McKenzie
Bob Kleier
Jim Skaggs
Col. Bob Spiller
Pipes Gaines
John Grider

Copyright © 2010, by Larry J. Pack
ISBN-13: 9780615396323
Library of Congress
Control Number 2010502550

Table of Contents

Prologue iv
About the Author vi
Credits vii
The Narrative
    I.   The 1920s 1
    II.   The 1930s 25
    III. The 1940s 47
    IV. The 1950s 59
    V.   The 1960s 65
    VI. The 1970s 73
    VII. The 1980s 81
    VIII. The 1990s 87
    IX. The 2000s 97
Epilogue 115
Profiles 117
Documents 153
The Press 173
The Presidents 189
The Gallery 195
Index of Members 227

Prologue

In writing this History of the Bowling Green Rotary Club (1920 - present) I have wanted to present the flavor and the spirit of the Club with the accuracy that any true history deserves. The history is written primarily for members past, present and future of the Club by a member who thinks he understands what the spirit of Rotary means to each of us.

The reader may think, at times, that the narrative contains too much minutia; but, I wanted, if possible, to have you and others experience the weekly luncheons anew and to feel the rhythm of the Club. You may also, at first, wonder why I included the extraneous material regarding other things that were impacting the world (including Rotary's world) at the same time. My thought was that these were frequently the things that were discussed at the tables during lunch. Some of these events were events that were uplifting to the whole society and other events, such as the wars, were events that touched the lives of the Rotarians and indeed all Americans. The events of World War II shaped almost every program leading up to the war, the war itself and the immediate post-war period. The patriotism of the Rotarians, as well as, the general populace was truly impressive - the war bond drives that Rotary participated in (I believe 8 in number) and the Clubs purchase of war bonds from the Club treasury showed real character. On one occasion, during the war, the Club had $1,274 left in the Treasury. It took $1,000 of this and bought another war bond, with no thought or worry of how depleting this might be to the treasury or of what other needs might come up.

The other wars impacted the Club less, perhaps, but impacted the families with family members involved 100%. You will note that I treated the Iraq and Afghanistan wars as a part of the War on Terror. They could have been treated separately. My treatment of them was not meant to make a judgment. Finally, about the wars and their impact on Rotary, I included the synopsis of each because even in 2009, most of the prayers at the noon luncheons involved a special petition for the American troops who were in harms way.

There is no difference in the importance of each Rotarian, but over the course of the Clubs history, there have been individuals who have served with such dedication and distinction that apart from the narrative, I have included a section to profile some of these members. Also, included are certain documents and representative newspaper articles, as well as, a list of present and former members, numbering about 700.

Also, from the very beginning in 1920, the relationship between Rotary and what is now Western Kentucky University and the Bowling Green Business University and College of Commerce is a relationship that is so intertwined and so symbiotic that they cannot be separated - even as these institutions and the Bowling Green community cannot be separated. The early leadership of Rotary especially involved almost giants from these institutions in the person of Dr. J. Lewie Harman, Sr., Dr. H.H. Cherry and J.Murray Hill, Sr. The influence of Western and the contribution it makes to Rotary and to the community and vice versa has continued through all the years of Rotary; even to the present time (2009). The Bowling Green Business University and the College of Commerce was melded into Western several years ago and continues its influence through Western.

It has been a great joy for me to discover and rediscover this history and I sincerely hope it will be for you. Enjoy.

Larry J. Pack

The Author

A native Kentuckian and life-time resident of Warren County, Dr. Larry Pack is particularly qualified to write what will surely become the definitive and insightful history of the Bowling Green Rotary Club. Educated in the Warren County public schools, the youthful Pack pursued his baccalaureate degree at nearby Western Kentucky State College (now Western Kentucky University) noted for its excellent program in pre-med and pre-dental training. After graduating in 1955 with a Bachelor of Science degree in biology, Pack spent two years on active military duty as an infantry officer, eventually earning the rank of captain in tbe Army Reserve.

In 1961, he married the former Peggy Ann Lewis of Bardstown, Kentucky while completing his Doctor of Dental Medicine degree from the University of Louisville. The next year he and Peggy settled in Bowling Green where they raised two children (Stephen Fielding and Julie Drew) and Larry began a forty-year practice of dentistry. Stephen is currently a successful architect in Chicago and Julie is a teacher and the wife of Rotarian Bruce Barrick. The Packs are also the proud grandparents of three promising young men. As a long-time resident of Bowling Green and active member of the Presbyterian Church, Dr. Pack was more than a successful and respected dentist; he was also a community leader and booster. Joining Rotary International in 1987, he became a Paul Harris Fellow and served as club president in 1999-2000. As president his accomplishments were many. He reinstituted both the popular Valentine's dinner-dance and the special recognition of member's birthdays, and he also encouraged the noon Rotary to finance and complete a Habitat for Humanity home in Bowling Green. An avid history buff himself, Dr. Pack, as monthly program chairman for three consecutive years, arranged for a popular series on our nation's outstanding presidents, led by history professors from WKU. As both a proud Rotarian and community leader, Dr. Pack has produced not only a comprehensive study of a local Rotary club but also an interesting account of how its members have enriched a city, a state, and a nation.

Robert V. Haynes
Professor Emeritus, WKU

Credits

Nancy Baird and Jonathan Jeffrey
The Kentucky Library

Dr. Robert V. Haynes
WKU History Professor

Sam C. Cook (Deceased) and Robert C. (Bob) Long
Past Secretaries of the Bowling Green Rotary Club

Alan Vilines
Present Secretary of the Bowling Green Rotary Club

Charles M. Moore, Jr.
Historian of the Bowling Green Rotary Club

Dr. J. Joe Cheek, Gary Dillard, Dr. Sally Ray, Col. Bob Spiller
Members of the Bowling Green Rotary Club

Major Ed Binnix
The Salvation Army and a Member of the Bowling Green Rotary Club

H.B. Clark
GSE Team Leader 1997 and a Member of the Bowling Green Rotary Club

Rob Porter
GSE Team Leader 2009 and a Member of the Bowling Green Rotary Club

Cora Jane Spiller
Wife of Rotarian Bob Spiller and History Buff

Rotary International
History/Rotary.org

J. Lewie Harman, Sr.
"A Brief Sketch of the Bowling Green Rotary Club" (1955)

Donna Hill
Formerly with the Kentucky Society of Crippled Children

Pat Ennis Reid
(Mrs. Charles Reid)
Granddaughter of W. Frank Ennis

Allen County Historical Society
Scottsville, Kentucky

The Medical Center
Bowling Green, Kentucky

The Depot and Railroad Museum
Bowling Green, Kentucky

Bowling Green City Hall
Bowling Green, Kentucky

Cliff Nahm
Great Great Grandson of Sam Nahm, Sr., Son of Frederick Nahm, Jr. and Marjorie Connerly Nahm

"Architecture of Warren County, Kentucky 1790-1940"
Published by Landmark Association of Bowling Green and Warren County Inc., 1984

Irene Moss Sumpter
Our Heritage - An Album of Early Bowling Green, Kentucky Landmarks

Kentucky State District Highway Office #3
Bowling Green, Kentucky

Herbert Oldham
Bowling Green Educator

Jonathan Jeffrey and Michael Dowell
"Bittersweet"

the 1920s

The Bowling Green Rotary Club met at the Farm Bureau on September 1, 1920, under the direction of Dr. Ed B. Rose, a Bowling Green dentist. Yet, it was at that point not a Rotary Club, but, rather fifteen Bowling Green citizens who had met for the purpose of forming a Rotary Club in Bowling Green. Dr. Rose was the authorized organizer. Rotary stipulated that to form a new club there had to be at least 15 charter members but not more than 25. At the organizational meeting, Dr. Rose presided and W.L. Craig was the acting Secretary. At this meeting the Constitution and By-laws were adopted and an executive committee was elected, consisting of J. Whit Potter, President; Dr.J.O. Carson, Vice President, and W.L. Craig, Secretary. Dr. F.D. Cartwright and A. Scott Hines were also on the executive committee. The executive committee immediately went into executive session and elected permanent officers. They were J. Whit Potter, a banker, President; J.O. Carson, an eye, ear, nose and throat physician, vice president; W.L. Craig, a college professor, secretary; and Harold W. Sublett, a pharmacist, treasurer. The charter members, besides the four officers, were: Dr. Fred Cartwright, general practice physician; Sterett Cuthbertson, dry goods; Samuel Cristal, produce; C.P. Evans, mail service; Guy H. Herdman, law; A. Scott Hines, wholesale grocer; Guy S. Jones, tobacco; S.K. Warrener, livestock; L. Mot Williams, men's clothing; and Ed Stout, real estate.

Potter was a member of the banking firm of Barclay and Potter located at 912 State Street.[1] This firm went through some name changes such as Potter-Matlock and Company in 1895 and Potter-Matlock Bank and Trust Company in 1905. Barclay and Potter had bought the 912 State location in 1897.

The 1920s

The Potter-Matlock name appeared later in a location at 431-437 E. 10th Avenue, known as the Cook Building. The final remnants of this name were merged into the American National Bank and Trust Company located at 922 State in 1958. The Whit Potter residence was located on the NW corner of State Street and 13th Street and has been completely restored to its original grandeur.[1] J. Whit Potter died in 1923.

The J.O. Carson offices were located at 442-444 East Main in the Barr Building. Carson and Dr. E.T. Barr, a dentist, shared the second floor of this building. E.T. Barr's son, Dr. E. Wallace Barr, later occupied this space.

W.L. Craig, a college professor, was head of the Science Department at Western Kentucky State Normal School. He was at Western for 46 years. W.L. Craig had a beautiful home built on Nashville Road in 1930. The home was located just south of University Boulevard.

Harold Sublett grew up on a farm 8 miles out Morgantown Road. He became associated with drug stores at an early age. He became a part of CDS, albeit, much later than Tibbis Carpenter and Emory G. Dent. The CDS firm was established in 1912. E.B. Stout was a realtor and Sam Cristal was in the produce business with his father-in-law, Sam Nahm, Sr.[19] The business was first located at 440 E. Main (on the square) in the Getty Building.[1] This building was, in contemporary times occupied by a Western Auto Store and later by 440 Restaurant. Of interest, this building has, even now, an intact roller-skating rink on its third floor. In 1875, Sam Cristal and Sam Nahm, Sr. moved their produce business to 827-829 State Street where it remained until 1947. This location is now occupied by Better Hearing Services. The Sam Cristal residence is located at 618 E. Main and is the former Presbyterian Manse.[1] Continuing on with charter members, A. Scott Hines was in the wholesale grocery business. Scott Hines was a brother-in-law of Duncan Hines. Duncan Hines, in 1936, wrote a book, entitled "Adventures in Good Eating."[11] The Duncan Hines name is still on many grocery products today. Scott Hines later served as Bowling Green's mayor from 1925-1929 and again in 1941-1942. Dr. Ed Rose, Rotary's organizer, was later named the Dean of the University of Tennessee's Dental School located at Memphis.

At that first organizational meeting, committees were named for entertainment and for membership. The entertainment committee was instructed to provide entertainment for a special meeting that was to be held in Bowling Green on September 16, 1920, at which District Governor C.W. Bailey and other Rotarians were to be invited. C.W. Bailey was from Clarksville, Tennessee and presented the Charter to the Club on November 24, 1920. The district, then, was composed of parts of Kentucky and Tennessee. It would go through several other name changes before it became 6710. The Bowling Green Club was the 771st club chartered. For a copy of the club's charter see the document section. The club was under the watchful eye of the Nashville, Tennessee Rotary Club. There was an application fee levied by Rotary of $25 for each 100 thousand population in the city in which the club was chartered. The minimum fee was $25; the maximum was $100. The club could not accept new members until its paper work was processed and approved by the parent organization. The club has had many meeting places in its ninety years of existence. As mentioned, the organizational meeting took place at the Farm Bureau offices. The luncheon meetings took place at locations such as the Dixie Café, located next to the Capitol Theater on East Main and then for several years the club met at the Presbyterian Church located on the SW corner of State Street and 10th Avenue. The ladies of the Church prepared the meal. They also met at the State Street Methodist Church located on the same corner location of State and 11th Avenues. The Morehead House, built in 1847, was another meeting place.[5] It was razed in 1923 and replaced by the beautiful Helm Hotel the same year. The Helm was a project of Rotary's Dr. T.O. Helm, classification hotel management. Later Cliff Lampkin became a Rotarian and was associated with the Helm. His classification too was ho-

> **CITIZENS NATIONAL SELECTS DIRECTORS**
>
> A meeting of the stockholders of the Citizens National Bank was held yesterday afternoon at the bank.
>
> Directors chosen to serve during the ensuing year are:
> Robert Rodes, R. W. Covington, M. B. Nahm, J. Murray Hill, E. G. Dent, T. O. Helm, Virgil Skiles, C. E. Francis, W. L. Matthews, B. J. Borrone and M. D. Alexander.
>
> *Park City Daily News 1/12/34*

tel management second to Dr. Helm. The Helm was the meeting place of Rotary for a longer period of time than all the other locations combined. It was razed in 1969 and replaced by the imposing new Citizens National Bank. Citizens had purchased the site a year earlier. The YMCA, located on the SE corner of State Street and 11th Avenue was another meeting place in those early years. The YMCA was built in 1909.[1] It had a reading room, gym, swimming pool, and a dorm. By 1918 the YMCA had 380 members. The building later was called the Downtown Hotel and still later the Park City Hotel. The Davenport building (also called the Neale Building) was located on the NW corner of State Street and 10th Avenue. That space is now occupied by the new BB&T Bank which faces Park Row, where Woolworths once stood. Rogers Tea Room, another meeting place was located on the NE corner of State Street and 10th Avenue where later the Herman Lowe Store was located. The Olde Fort Restaurant located on old 31-W between the College Street bridge and where the road joins the newer 31-W after crossing the Emory G. Dent Bridge was a stone structure where Rotary met for several years. The Olde Fort burned in November of 1961. There was a second Rotary meeting place that burned – this was the Kentucky Belle Restaurant located on 8th Avenue behind what is now Mariah's. The Kentucky Belle was in part a replica of the Belle of Louisville. The Kentucky Belle burned in February of 1973. The fire destroyed the flag collection of Rotary that had been started by the late Rotarian, Dr. L.O.

Toomey. Dr. Toomey was a world traveler. Over the years, the flag collection has been built up again. The club then moved to the College Street Inn, which had become institutionalized over the years by several generations of young people. It was owned and operated by Herb and Maxine Lowe. The club met for a short time at the College Street Towers and then at the Executive Inn which was located at the SE corner of Scottsville Road and Alvaton Road (Ken Bale Boulevard) and Three Springs Road. The site is the location of the new Olive Garden Restaurant. Rotary seems to have found its home at the Bowling Green Country Club, off Beech Bend Road, where it has met for the last several years.

The local club hit the ground running. At the April 20, 1921 meeting, the motion was made to purchase property for a permanent campground for the Boy Scouts of America. This project was assigned to the Boys Work Committee. In May of 1921, the Club paid $200 down for a site on Ewings Ford Road but due to not being able to get a clear title to that property, the purchase was scuttled. The second attempt to purchase a site was more productive. The site was located on Scottsville Road about one mile beyond where the twin bridges are now located on what was and is Collet Road. That would have been about 8 miles from the Broadway, Smallhouse, Covington Avenue intersection. The campsite, itself, was located at the bottom of a steep bluff on Drakes Creek. The incline of the bluff was about 60 degrees. The flat area campsite would have been perhaps between one and two acres. Drakes Creek in that area was deep enough to furnish a great swimming hole – deep enough for diving. There was also an enormous spring upstream, maybe a hundred yards that channeled into the creek. Over the next couple of years, the club voted to build a road down the bluff to the camp. This was done on the recommendation of the Committee on Boys Work. That Boys Work Committee was composed of Ed. Rose, Chairman, Frank Ennis, W. L. Craig, Mot Williams and W.L. Sibert. However, Frank Ennis seems to have become chair (de facto) because of the tremendous amount of know-how that he exhibited. This was probably due to the background knowledge that he possessed. Frank Ennis classification in Rotary was cut stone and concrete. He had done the concrete work on the YMCA in 1908-1909, City Hall in 1907 and First Baptist Church in 1913-1915. The Church building was the third building for the congregation. It burned October 14, 1991. The present First Baptist Church building dedicated December 18, 1994 is the fourth and followed the burning of the third. So, Frank Ennis was in his natural element developing the Rotary Camp.

Frank Ennis was the father of Noel Ennis, Sr. who also continued the concrete business and the grandfather of Rotarian Noel Ennis, Jr.[6] The road to the camp was built down the bluff and there would have been numerous dynamite blasts necessary to remove rock that would have been almost solid in places. The road was eventually graded, drained and graveled, remaining a gravel road as long as Rotary owned the property. Keep in mind that all of this occurred within a year or two of the Club being chartered. Rotary owned the camp for many years and operated it as a Boy Scout Camp as well as a place to have many enjoyable outings for the Club. We will have much more to say about the camp as we go along. Today, 2009, Rotarian Bob Hovius and his wife Sandra have a beautiful home that sits atop the bluff and overlooks the old campsite as well as Drakes Creek (Bob joined Rotary in 1967 and is still an active member).

The earliest mention of Emory G. Dent was that he addressed the club at its meeting on September 29, 1921 on the subject of road building in Kentucky. Emory Dent was a force in Rotary and a successful businessman (he was the Dent in Carpenter, Dent, Sublett drug store chain), but the overriding lifetime interest of this man was road-building. Remember his name because he stands very near the pinnacle of what members of the local club have been able to accomplish. At the January 4, 1922 meeting, which was held at the YMCA, three new members were introduced – all of whom would impact the club. They were Henry Hardin Cherry, President of Western Kentucky State Normal School, George Moseley, local businessman and J.L. Harman, Sr., vice president of the Bowling Green Business University.

On January 17, 1922, the Club met in the new dining room of the Presbyterian Church, located at State Street and 10th Avenue. The ladies of the Church prepared and served the meal. This would be home to the Club for the foreseeable future. It was a good relationship for the Club and for the ladies of the church. They (the ladies) ended up using the money they made to buy the bell for the Church. On April 22, 1922 the club elected new officers for the 1922-1923 Rotary year. Dr. J.O. Carson, the Vice President, was elected President; A. Scott Hines, Vice President; W.J. Craig, re-elected Secretary; and Harold Sublett, Treasurer. Dr. Carson appointed chairs for the following committees: Fellowship, Public Welfare, Boys Works (Frank Ennis), Education and Entertainment. J.L. Harman, Sr. addressed the Club on the Bowling Green Business University. Remember J.L. Harman, W.S. Ashley and J.S. Dickey had purchased the Business University from H.H. Cherry when he moved the Southern Normal School to the hilltop in 1906 and it became Western Kentucky State Normal School with Dr. Cherry as President. J.S. Dickey became President of the Business University and served in that capacity until 1921 when J.L. Harman became President.

At the May 17, 1922 meeting, Rotarian Sam Cristal, partner with Sam Nahm, Sr. in the produce business, now located at 823 State (formerly at 440 E. Main) reported on the work being done to secure the funds to build a lodge at the Drakes Creek campsite.

It was in this timeframe that the committee on Boys Work reported that the Club should receive the deed to the property within the next two weeks. In August of 1922, the grounds were being improved and $200 was appropriated to build the road down the bluff to the campsite.

At the November 22, 1922 meeting Rotarian Dr. J.O. Carson gave a mesmerizing report on a little crippled girl whom he had seen while on a family trip out in the county. The child was able to move only on all fours. It was a report that touched the individual Club members; hence was born the Crippled Children's Committee, which is still functioning in contemporary times. Within a month, the child had been sent to Louisville for evaluation. Mrs. Max B. Nahm was instrumental in getting her clothes and preparing her for the trip. The Louisville doctors' report was that she indeed could be helped to the degree of enabling her to walk and lead a useful life.

On February 7, 1923, the first of many Ladies Nights was held. It celebrated the 19th anniversary of the founding of Rotary. Eighty-four Rotarians and guests attended the evening social. Eleven days later the Club held a memorial meeting to lament the death of J. Whit Potter, charter member and the Club's first charter member to die.

The committee system seemed to work almost to perfection. Now, in the general culture, we say "if you want to kill a proposal – appoint a committee," but in 1923 with Rotary only three years old it was thriving by using the committee system for getting things done and it had been the case since the inception of the local Club, when a committee was appointed for Boys Work. Nineteen twenty-three was fairly routine with different committees reporting. Emory Dent, Chair of Crippled Children's Committee, on March 28, 1923 reported on the work being done by the Louisville hospital for crippled children. In April 1923, committees for the following Rotary year were named by the new President, A.S. Hines. There was a committee for Entertainment, a Committee for Fellowship, one for Education, chaired by Dr. J. L. Harman, President of the Business University, of course, one for Boys Work, a committee for Public Welfare, chaired by H.H. Cherry, President of the State Normal School, one for International Relations and one for Publicity.

In May 1923, the Club was informed that the Rotary Camp needed $1500 for permanent equipment. A campaign was instituted to raise the money. At the June 2, 1923 meeting, the executive committee proposed rules for selecting new members, and the club decided to meet June 24th at the Boy Scout Camp. At the next meeting, the Club's own Dr. Cartwright was the forerunner of our own Dr. Ken Embrey who gave free flu shots in the first decade of the 21st century. Typhoid was a prevalent disease in 1923 and maybe swimming in the Drakes Creek and drinking water out of the campground spring were incentives for a little preventive medicine.

In the summer of that year, the Club endorsed its first of several bond issues to build a new hospital. The bond issue was for $130,000.

Later in 1923, a memorial meeting was held for President Warren G.

> ## City Hospital
>
> **1926:** The original city hospital was built in 1926 on Reservoir Hill at a cost of $130,000. The hill had served as the College Hill Fort during the Civil War in 1861 when Bowling Green was briefly named the capital of the Confederacy.
>
> **1946:** The hospital had outgrown its facility. A city ordinance was passed for expansion to accommodate 100-125 patients. A land transaction was granted to Warren County and the hospital became known as BG-Warren Co. Hospital.
>
> **1952:** On September 10, 1952, the dedication and cornerstone ceremonies were held. 1,800 people attended.
>
> **1972:** There was a 32,000 square foot addition.
>
> **1977:** 21 acres on High Street was purchased to locate a new facility.
>
> **1978:** Through reorganization the name was changed to the Medical Center.
>
> **1980:** On March 8, the hospital moved from Reservoir Hill to its new location and facilities on Park Street. Now functioning as the Medical Center, it has continued to expand and diversify. It is now a major medical center. [18]

Harding. That, of course, was before so much polarization had become a part of the national dialogue.

As September 1923 approached, the birdhunters in the club were instructed to bring in enough birds next week to feed the Club. The ladies prepared the birds. I assume that these were the ladies of the Presbyterian Church since that is where they were meeting and also assume the birds were doves since the dove-hunting season opens September first.

On October 24, 1923, Dr. H.H. Cherry, President of Western Kentucky Normal School and Teacher's College of Bowling Green gave the program, which was an explanation of the Normal Heights Foundation. He explained its benefits. Extrapolation would indicate that this foundation was ultimately to become the College Heights Foundation as it passed through its name changes. At the end of October 1923, the Club had 56 members and 50 of them were in attendance at the October 24, 1923 meeting for a percentage of the memberships in attendance of 90%. As the culture has changed, so has the attendance.

Bowling Green looked like it was on a roll during the roaring 20s, and all boats were lifted – including Rotary's. At the end of October 1923 a new hotel was under construction. Later that year T.O. Helm was elected to membership in Rotary, and his classification was hotel management. One hundred and seventy-five dollars was voted to improve the Rotary/Boy Scout camp.

There were some lighter things happening too, although they were probably serious to the members of 1923. The National Fox Hunters Association was to be invited to hold their next meeting in Bowling Green. One can imagine that the late Judge Robert Coleman would have been elated. Judge Coleman was the father of our own Rotarian Ward Coleman. Ward joined Rotary on April 1, 1999.

Also, a committee was appointed to improve the mule trade in Bowling Green. Nineteen twenty-three ended with Dr. H.H. Cherry discussing the hardships of Western State Normal School. Two years later Rotarian H.H. Cherry would assume the Presidency of Rotary – its 5th President. Early in 1924, state legislators would visit Western to make an on site inspection preparatory to the appropriation of funds. Had that been today, our own Representative Jody Richards would have led the charge as he has done so many times in the years that he has served – especially as Speaker of the House (Jody Richards joined the Rotary on 10/17/84). The movement to make Mammoth Cave a National Park heated up in 1924. The Club endorsed the movement to build a road from Mammoth Cave to the "Outside World," and on May 7, 1924, John B. Rodes spoke to Rotary on the movement to make Mammoth Cave a national park. It was pointed out that the cave is one of the seven original Wonders of the New World. Later, Rotarian Dr. J.L. Harman personally lobbied President Calvin Coolidge to give favorable consideration to the Mammoth Cave National Park Bill. Bowling Green businessman Max

Nahm was very instrumental in this process. John B Rodes was mayor of Bowling Green from 1929-1933 and later was a very distinguished Warren County Circuit Judge.

On June 24, 1924, the Club was apprised that the sign for the Rotary Boy Scout Camp had been placed at the gate to the Camp on Collett Road near Alvaton and was ready for inspection. Also, the Club was notified that membership in the Crippled Children's Society would remain at $2.00 per member per year.

On September 24, 1924, the ladies of the Presbyterian Church informed

Urges Formation Of Crippled Children's Commission Here

2/22/39

Miss Marian Williamson, director of the Kentucky Crippled Children's Commission, addressed the Rotary Club at its weekly luncheon-meeting today at the Helm hotel and presented plans for the organization of a Warren county committee to work with the state society.

In attendance at the meeting were representatives of the Lions club, Kiwanis club, Elks Lodge, Business and Professional Women's Club, American Legion, Community Chest, Chamber of Commerce, and other civic organizations.

The Rotary club, a member of the state society, agreed to sponsor the project which was presented by Sam Cristal, chairman of the club's crippled children's committee, who in turn introduced Emory G. Dent. The county organization, to be known as the Warren County Crippled Children's Society, has as its chairman, Sam Cristal, and its vice-chairman, Mrs. Bert R. Smith. Other officers are W. W. Holman, secretary, and Roy Cooksey, treasurer.

The directors are Mrs. Hallie Baumberger, Evan C. Evans, J. A. Bryant, James Gorin, Gaston Cole, W. L. Stevens and J. P. Masters. Committee chairmen are as follows: Transportation, Fred Nahm; clinics, Dr. G. M. Wells; membership, H. St. G. T. Carmichael; education, L. C. Curry; vocational rehabilitation, L. T. Smith; publicity, John Gaines, John Ditto and J. G. Denhardt; legislation, E. G. Dent; co-ordination, W. T. Stowe.

Visitors at the meeting today, in addition to Miss Williamson, were Miss Gene Merrill, also of the Kentucky Crippled Children's Commission, Louisville; the Rev. Andy Newcomer of Auburn, W. R. Borches of Nashville, S. C. Harlin of Glasgow, and Mr. and Mrs. Bert R. Smith, Mrs. J. G. Woodruff, Mrs. Hallie Baumberger, Miss Josephine Lindsay, Miss Daisy Black, H. St. G. T. Carmichael, Preston C. Haynes, Harold H. Huffman, Dr. L. K. Causey, Evan C. Evans, J. P. Masters, John C. Davis, W. T. Stowe, Dr. W. R. McCormack, T. T. Elkins, Dr. W. O. Carson, H. E. Elrod, Dr. John H. Blackburn, W. L. Stevens, Dr. W. J. Edens, Dr. V. Graham, Dr. G. M. Wells, Fred Nahm, J. A. Bryant, Paul F. Kimbrough, Arnold Winkenhofer, L. Y. Lancaster, N. Y. Landrum, Frank L. Strange, Gaston W. Cole, Dr. C. E. Francis, Dr. Charles B. Stovall, the Rev. Dr. A. B. Houze, Roger M. Parrish, Jr., V. P. Cassaday and H. J. Guttman.

The 1920s

the Club that they were giving up serving the Club. The Club advised the membership that beginning October 1, 1924, they would meet at the Helm Hotel. There were to be many many changes in meeting places.

Ladies night was held December 12, 1924. Sons and daughters of Rotarians were invited to attend the dance after the parents had finished dinner. This was the first of numerous times that sons and daughters were invited near Christmas. It was probably the forerunner of the Annual Christmas Party with Santa that we enjoy today, but anything closely resembling our Christmas Party was to wait until 1936.

In January 1925, it was announced that a Crippled Children's Clinic would be held in Bowling Green. This clinic was not to be held until May 25, 1926. It was the first of what would be the numerous clinics to be held in Bowling Green, all of which were held at the Presbyterian Church.

In 1925, Dr. H.H. Cherry became President of Rotary. Concurrently, a new Kentucky-Tennessee district was named and an innovation that still continues was announced. Identification badges were to be made and placed at the door of the meeting room. In May of 1925, Dr. Cherry invited the Club to hold its next meeting at Western Kentucky State Normal School and Teachers College on May 24th. It was the first of many such occasions. In 2009, Rotarian Dr. Nathan Hodges invited the Club to have lunch at the Culinary School, a part of KETAC, of which he is President. The lunch and

Courtesy of Kentucky Library
Mansard Hotel

From 1847, when the Morehead House was built at State and Main Streets, until 1970 when the Helm Hotel was razed this corner was for one hundred and three years the location of the leading hotel in the city of Bowling Green. The hotel derived its name from Charles D. Morehead and members of the family were proprietors until 1862 when it was purchased by Mrs. John Hess. When built by James K. McGoodwin it was a two-story brick structure and more or less patterned after the Younglove building, across the way, with a palladian window, above the second story, between two large chimneys built flush with the wall. The Younglove building, from which it was patterned, is still standing and houses the Williams Drug Store. At the death of Mrs. Hess in 1876 the management soon fell to her three daughters, Camilla (Mrs. John N. Herdman), Julie (Mrs. Dewey) and Sarah E. (Mrs. Valerius Armitage).

In 1915 the Morehead House was purchased by Dr. T.O. Helm. By 1919 because of a large oil boom in the area the hotel business also boomed and in 1923 Dr. Helm razed the old Morehead House and built a new modern structure naming it appropriately The Helm Hotel. The new hotel was the center of all civic and social life of the city for many years. In 1969 it was purchased by the Citizens National Bank, razed and their beautiful new Bank constructed on the lot in 1970.

the meeting were great and at least reminded this Rotarian of that original invitation by Dr. Cherry.

The Club bulletin, "the Pinion," was introduced in this timeframe. The "Pinion" had starts and stops and more changes through the years before finally becoming "The Cog" about 1961. "The Pinion" was definitely the forerunner of all the others. I wondered about the choice of the name Pinion and found that it means "a small cog (toothed) wheel that interdigitates with a larger wheel as it turns" – sounds appropriate. The committees continued to function - Boys Work, Crippled Children, Attendance, Entertainment, etc.

At that first Crippled Children's Clinic that was held on May 25, 1926, there were 108 children examined and all but 20 could be helped – a phenomenal percentage – a phenomenal reward for Rotary's effort and a tremendous hope for the affected children.

Earlier in 1925, it was evident how much was going on in Bowling Green. Bowling Green High School had been started in 1908. Two new Ogden College Buildings were in the works. [5] Funds had already been subscribed. Bonds for the aforementioned new hospital were to be voted on in the next election, and the new railroad depot, located at 4th and Kentucky Streets would be dedicated on October 1, 1925, after having been in the works for almost 24 years. Rotary, on at least two occasions, had envisioned a "great white way" from the depot to Fountain Square. But before there was a railroad going through Bowling Green there was a Portage Railroad. [4] The Portage Railroad, near what is now the Boatlanding, was originated by local businessmen J. Rumsey Skiles. Skiles sold $20,000 worth of stock to finance the Portage Railroad. He had a three-acre tract near the Boatlanding where the Railroad originated. The railroad was constructed with wood timbers with metal strips fastened to them. There were no cross ties. Horses pulled tram cars along these strips to a location where the Warren County Courthouse now stands where Skiles owned another three acre tract. The Courthouse was still in Fountain Square Park. The Railroad ran parallel to Church Street to the intersection of Main and Adams Streets. The Portage then ran between Adams and Kentucky Streets to 10th Avenue and then to the present Warren County Courthouse site. The Portage Railroad was completed in 1837. Later the James Rumsey

The 1920s

Skiles mansion "Kinloch" was built near the river. It was a short distance from "Riverview" which is at the foot of Main Street. Construction of Riverview [1] was halted during the Civil War when Confederate forces occupied Bowling Green. The mansion was completed after the War. The house was one of the most sophisticated designs in 19th century Warren County. The house is a public treasure today and is open to the public. James Rumsey Skiles donated land for the Presbyterian Church which is located at State and 10th Avenue from that original Portage tract.[1] The Church was constructed in 1833 and is of Gothic revival architecture. It precedes by 15 years any other church in Kentucky with this architectural design. It is possible that a central core of the building was built and the exterior design later. Originally the church had been located on the Southwest corner of Repose Park (Pioneer Cemetery). Repose Park[1] is located at College Street between 5th and 6th Avenue. The Cemetery was established on land donated by Bowling Green pioneer Robert Moore about 1817. It was known as Repose Park in 1877. It was the city's first public cemetery and was used until the 1860s when Fairview Cemetery was opened. Many of the area's earliest pioneers were buried here, including Robert Moore. The church congregation was founded in 1819. The original church was thought to have burned in 1830 or 1831. For a few years between 1835 and 1846 the Bowling Green Female Academy was conducted in the basement of the church where the Bowling Green Rotary Club held many of its early luncheons. During the Civil War, the doors and windows were removed and the church was used as a hospital. Later additions to the church include a pastor's study in 1890 and a women's parlor and choir loft were included in a 1921 renovation. An educational wing was added in 1949 and the Cook building, facing 10th Street behind the church and adjacent to the Courthouse was purchased in 1961. The Cook building was razed in 1991 and the present educational building and church offices were constructed.[7] This building is a key structure in the architectural history of the downtown district. It is the only remaining church in the historic core of downtown. There was a time when the manse was located at the rear of the church.

On June 24, 1925, President Cherry appointed a committee to explore bringing a branch of the Pet Milk Company to Bowling Green. On July 15,

1925, S.C. (Sam) Cook was to succeed W.J. Craig as the second secretary of the Bowling Green Rotary Club. It would have been unimaginable, at that time, to think that Sam would serve in that capacity for 46 years. Sam Cook's records are the source of much of the information in this history coupled with the records of our own Bob Long, who succeeded Sam in 1971. We will have more to say about both of these men later.

On August 19, 1925, Rotarian, Dr. J.L. Harman, invited the Club to attend commencement at the Business University.

The New Training School at Western was to be dedicated on October 30, 1925. Evidently, the ladies of the Presbyterian Church had a change of mind because on October 28, 1925 the Club was back at the church for meetings and meals.

The present depot located at 4th and Center Streets was in the mill for 24 years but was finally opened at dedication ceremonies on October 1, 1925. Carl D. Herdman who bought the first ticket, owned and operated the Morehead House. The Morehead House was Bowling Green's foremost 19th century hotel in the 1870s. The L & N Railroad was completed to Bowling Green in 1859. The first station and round house were located at Main and Adams Streets. The new 1925 depot was to serve the city until 1979 when passenger service was discontinued. The depot was boarded up for many years and fell into disrepair; but, thanks to the city fathers and many interested citizens, renovations occurred from 1995 to 2007 in phases. Today, there is a Railroad Museum and many other historical entities, including six fully restored railcars. These railcars include a locomotive, a presidential office car, a pullman, a diner, a railway post office car and a caboose. The depot is open to the public and is a great testimonial to the past and the present and to what interested, hardworking citizens can accomplish.[8]

Back to James Rumsey Skiles and the downtown tract of the Portage Railroad where the Warren County Courthouse was constructed. The Courthouse, located at 425 E. 10th Avenue, was built in 1868-1869 and was designed by architect D.J. Williams. It is of Italinate design. It is second only, in the state, to the Jefferson County Courthouse in Louisville. This Courthouse replaced the previous one located in Fountain Square Park. The first, a log courthouse was later replaced with a brick structure. The stone for the present Warren County Courthouse was quarried from Warren County. The cupola has been reconstructed twice in the 20th century following fires. It nearly duplicates the original. Local architect Creedmore Fleener was responsible for alterations after the first fire. The exterior, including the iron and stone fence, has been preserved in its originality.[1]

According to the "Pinion" of May 25, 1925, Dr. Cherry appointed Emory G. Dent Chair of the Crippled Children's Committee. Emory Dent chaired the Committee for several years and did an outstanding job. After all bills were paid and the accounts audited for the 1924-1925, (after the District conference in Louisville in March) the committee in charge found a balance of $1,024.07. The balance was divided into thirds and given to:

The Tennessee Society for Crippled Children.
The Kentucky Society for Crippled Children.
Boys Work Committee of Louisville Rotary.

Late in 1925 and early 1926 saw new members introduced to the Club that would greatly impact the Club's future. The two new members were J. Lewie Harmon, Sr. and J. Murray Hill, Sr. Ward Sumpter was a guest.

Emory Dent, chair of Crippled Children's Committee, reported on a child whose last name was Lamastus that the Club had helped and read a "thank you" note from the child's family. He also asked Rotary's own Dr. Fred Cartwright (a charter member) to check on a child named Doc Hood who lived at 224 High Street and report to the Club on his condition.

On December 30, 1925, Dr. T.O. Helm announced that a Rotary School would be held at the Helm on January 4th-6th, 1926. This was probably the earliest reference to what we now call orientation for new members.

In early February of 1926, Guy Byrne, Chair of Community Services Committee, assured the Club that the new College Street Bridge across Barren River would be open on March 1, 1926. The College Street Bridge is the oldest standing bridge to span Barren River. It was the principal approach to the city from the north; and, it indeed was opened on that date. Prior to that date there were at least three other bridges that occupied that site. A

The 1920s

bridge built circa 1819 was replaced with a covered bridge built in 1838. This covered bridge burned February 14, 1862. Another covered bridge which was built after 1873, burned February 12, 1915. The present stone pylon was built for the 1838 bridge. The College Street Bridge is now a pedestrian walkway, and was refurbished for that purpose in 1992. The refurbishment was a joint project by the local district office of the Kentucky State Highway Department and local businessman and former Rotarian David Garvin.[9]

The election of officers for the Club was done very differently in the early years; and, indeed all the years, until the late 1980s or early 1990s. Someone, in the Club would nominate the entire Club roster for directors. When the vote was counted, the six or seven with the most votes would meet and elect a president, a vice president, a secretary and a treasurer. The remainder would serve as directors. This convention was the norm until in recent years when the incoming president selects his or her choice for one new director. A couple of weeks later, the Club votes on all the new officers, including confirmation of the new Director. This way, the senior director, becomes President each year, and there is always experienced leadership.

On May 26, 1926, Congressman Alben W. Barkley spoke to the Club on the subject of Crippled Children. One would have thought he would have been a guest of Emory Dent, but he was a guest of H.H. Cherry. During the middle months of 1926 there were numerous discussions relating to the Boys Work Committee; specifically to the Rotary Boy Scout Camp property. Additional funds for maintenance and improvements at the site were always needed. On August 26th of 1926 the Club met at the camp on Drakes Creek. Swimming, boating and games were a part of this meeting and were followed by a delicious meal with wives and friends present.

In June of 1926, the matter of singing at the weekly meetings was discussed and President Frank Cole instructed the Music Committee to be prepared to sing at least two songs at each weekly meeting. This was the first instance of singing at the meetings, but it seemed to institutionalize the practice. Later, the Club would have Mrs. Nell Gooch Travelstead of Western to lead the singing. Also, the Club hired a pianist for accompaniment. In recent times, the Club has treated singing at the meetings more or less as a joke until

2009 when President Mays has offered some encouragement to the practice and our own Dr. Janet Smith began very ably to lead the singing. To the untrained ear, the Club sounds pretty good. Let's return to Mrs. Travelstead. Many of us who attended Western State College in the 1950s remember the compulsory chapel on Wednesday mornings. Dean Finley C. Grise (grandfather of our own Judge John Grise) chaired the chapel program and Mrs. Nell Gooch Travelstead led the singing of (among other numbers), "Oh College Heights." Anyway, the paid song leader and pianist survived until the depression years of the 1930s when the Club had to tighten its belt, financially, as did everyone else, and the Club, I'm sure reluctantly, let them go.

MORNINGSTAR
The Lecturer
Wednesday, August 27, 3:30 P. M.

Actually, singing in Rotary was introduced on the national level much earlier than the above related experience in our own Club. Here's how it occurred. Paul Harris and four others met on February 23, 1905. Paul Harris was a lawyer, Silvester Scheele, a coal dealer; Gustavous E. Lehr, mining engineer, and E. Shorey, a merchant tailor. They met at the office of Gustavous E. Lehr, which by today's standard would have been considered drab – then it was pretty much standard. The next day, a future member of this group met with them. His name was Harry Ruggles, a printer. It was Ruggles, who at an early meeting, jumped upon a chair and shouted, "let's sing."

In August 1926, Cliff Lampkin was elected to membership second to Dr Helm in hotel management. Dr. Helm had recently represented the Club at the Rotary International Convention, in Denver. Cliff Lampkin would later serve as mayor of Bowling Green.

On August 25, 1926, F.F. Pepper of Greer Furniture rendered an excellent program demonstrating the orthophonic victrola. Maybe that would have been equivalent to Rotary's own Henry Pepper playing the handsaw (joined Rotary 7/16/1969). Henry has presented this program twice in recent years and he can almost make the saw talk.

On September 22, 1926, Bob Morningstar, formerly of Bowling Green and later of Chicago, gave the program. Bob was associated with the Chatauqua movement which involved summer schools and correspondence schools inaugurated at Chatauqua Lake, New York in 1874. These educational and recreational assemblies were composed of lectures, concerts, etc. Bob was the grandfather of Cora Jane Morningstar Spiller, wife of our own Col. Bob Spiller (joined Rotary 12/10/1980), and the father-in-law of Cora Jane Morningstar, reporter and city editor of the Daily News. (Bob Morningstar's picture is on the facing page).

At the November 26, 1926 meeting, the Club voted $25 per month for needy children in the Bowling Green Public School System. This work had previously been done by the Welfare Home. Related to this, the Club asked the school system to select 49 boys who were deficient in some way and needed personal attention and encouragement. Why the number 49? It was because the Club had 50 members at that time. This was probably the first mentoring program for Rotary and portended a much more extensive mentoring program during the 1990s forward that was an essential part of the Adopt-a-Class Program.

Nineteen twenty-seven started out with a Ladies Night Social on January 29th. This event had been a part of the local Club almost from the beginning. It was a wonderful recognition of the wives and a much looked forward to social event for both Rotarians and wives. It was to be another 64 years before the local Club would have women members. On February 23, 1927, our Rotary Club sent a telegram offering congratulations to coach Ed Diddle of Western Kentucky State Teachers College, who was in a basketball tournament at Winchester.

As the decade of the 20s wound down, the Club was again meeting at the Presbyterian Church. Whenever summer approached, thoughts turned again to the Rotary Camp and the fun outings that Rotary had enjoyed there. A new dining hall had been built together with a kitchen and several bunk houses. The work had been completed and Rotary was to have its June 19, 1929 meeting at the Camp. Later in the summer, a watermelon feast was

The 1920s

held in the same location. Most likely, the watermelons were chilled in the campground spring located on the property. The portends of the Depression were beginning to be brought into the Club's consciousness and money adjustments, brought about by necessity. On an upbeat note, it was announced that J. Murray Hill, Sr. would run for district governor.

The contacts with Coach Diddle continued for many years; usually involving the National Invitational Tournament and afterward within the next few weeks, he and Mr. Hornback would bring some of the team members to do the Rotary program or at least to be guests. Even in contemporary times the Club responds well to the coaches and players from WKU being guests of the Club.

On June 19, 1927 the meeting was turned into a 4th of July celebration. Rodes K. Myers, a local attorney and future Lt. Governor of the State of Kentucky, as well as a famous defense attorney addressed the Club. The Club, in unison, renewed their pledge to the flag. The program was closed by a solo of the Star-Spangled Banner by Uncle Billy Hill and a closing prayer by Parson George Cheek. I asked our own Dr. Joe Cheek (joined Rotary 1-3-1962) if the Reverend Cheek was related. Apparently he was not an ancestor of Joe's, but he knew about him.

On July 13, 1927 the Club met at the Helm Hotel and the music was furnished by the hotel orchestra. You are probably as amazed as I that the Hotel had an orchestra.

At that same meeting, Bill Richeson told about having recently flown from Louisville to Memphis in one of Henry Ford's planes. He again brought up the subject of a landing field for Bowling Green and greatly encouraged the same. On July 28, 1927, the meeting was held at Chalybeate Springs. After dinner, some of the members participated in a fox hunt, others danced, while still others enjoyed the restfulness of the springs. On the first meeting in August, President Frank Cole asked the Club to request the District Governor to hold a school for presidents and secretaries in Bowling Green – hence the probable beginning of the "PETS" meetings which two officers still attend each year. Professor J. Murray Hill, Sr. had a student of the Business University, from Hattiesburg, Mississippi as a guest. This, too, was a portent of the future of The Business University when numerous students from Mississippi would one by one become students and graduates of the Bowling Green Business University.

We would be remiss if we did not mention a great national and international event that took place earlier in 1927. At 7:52 am on May 20, 1927 the "Spirit of St. Louis," an aircraft piloted by Charles A. Lindberg, took off from Garden City, New York for the first ever transatlantic flight. Lindberg was not only the pilot but also the sole occupant of the single engine aircraft. He landed at Bourget Field, near Paris, on May 21, 1927 at 10:21 pm (5:21 pm Eastern Time). He had flown 3600 miles in 33 hours and 30 minutes. As we said before, this was one of the (probably the most) exhilarating things that impacted upon the national and world psyche in the late 20s. In 1932, Amelia Earhart would be the first woman to do the same. She flew from Harbor Grace Newfoundland to Ireland.

In October 1927 the Club had an appointment to sell part of the Rotary Camp. President Cole and the Board were authorized to negotiate the sale; on November 30th the negotiations were completed and the Club voted to sell the first part for $250 down and four notes of $250 each.

On November 2nd President H.H. Cherry announced "Homecoming" at Western and the football game between Western and U of L. The Club voted to participate in the raising of two million dollars for the Mammoth Cave Project. The Round Table Committee functioned as an advisory committee on roads to the cave and also a road to the Pet Milk Company.

During this general period James M. Hill and Lon Causey were approved for membership. Lon Causey's classification was telegraph and cable services. Marshall Love Sr. was congratulated on the birth of a son, Marshall Love. Jr. Marshall Love, Sr. operated the Marshall Love Office and School Supply in the 400 Block of E. Main. Later the business was on the 400 block of E. 10th Avenue across from the Courthouse. In May of 1928, H.H. Donovan, President of Eastern Kentucky State Normal School, was a guest of Dr. Cherry. Later H.H. Donovan would be President of the University of Kentucky at Lexington.

In early May of 1928, past District Governor Coleman Taylor informed the Club that Charter Night for the Auburn Club would be July 13th and for the Glasgow Club July 19th.

On July 18, 1928, Emory Dent told the Club about his trip around the world. In the following years, Emory Dent would make 3 other trips around the world.

At the September 19, 1924 meeting the Club contributed $50 to the road fund to build a road from Plano (now 622) to Alvaton. This road would be a straight line between two points as opposed to the winding route taken by the existing Frank Collett Road. It would also involve building two new bridges across Drakes Creek. As a benefit to Rotary, it would go within a couple hundred feet or so of the Rotary Camp on Collett road. This road, if built, would practically eliminate thru traffic on Old Scottsville Road. Today, Old Scottsville road is one of the most beautiful roads in Warren County. It has the same topography as it did in 1928 and its scenic beauty is unsurpassed. It looks like a country lane. Later that year Emory Dent announced a campaign run by the state to raise $100,000 for Crippled Children.

On October 31, 1928 it was moved to contribute $200 each year for 5 years to the Western Kentucky State Teachers College Scholarship Fund. The fund was to be known as the Foundation Fund. Almost surely, it was another step toward the College Heights Foundation of which Rotary has had such close relationship – especially in recent years through Rotary's own Alex Downing and before that with the fund's previous director and former President of Western, the beloved Dero Downing. In December 1928, Harold Sublett, one of our Charter members, resigned and later in the month George Mosely talked to the Club again about an airport and a road to the Pet Milk Plant.

Harry Spillman of New York City ushered in the last year of the decade as guest speaker.[3] Mr. Spillman, a native of Scottsville was a noted author and speaker. This would be the first of numerous times he would deliver the program. Spillman was born April 27, 1882 in Scottsville, Kentucky. He was one of Allen County's favorite sons. At age 18, he was a reporter for the local newspaper (census of 1900) and ten years later (census of 1910) he was a teacher in the local school system. At some point, he migrated to New York

City and worked for the Remington-Rand Typewriter Company as a motivational speaker. He traveled worldwide after becoming a noted author and lecturer. Six times in 17 years he spoke to the Bowling Green Rotary Club, when home visiting his sister Jessie and a host of Scottsville friends. At this January 1929 meeting, he was a guest of Rotarian J. Lewie Harman, Sr. In 1945, he was an honorary pallbearer for noted Rotarian Emory G. Dent.

These very early years of the Bowling Green Rotary Club were truly amazing, and it was populated by some great men. One wonders if because of their great strengths and drive did they make Rotary great or conversely because of the values that Rotary stood for and articulated did Rotary contribute to their greatness? One, perhaps, always wonders when one sees great leadership – do events make the man or does man make the events?

Early on, it looked like the men in The Bowling Green Rotary Club invented the phrase "Service Above Self." They certainly lived it each day. But for the record, I checked with the History and Archives section of Rotary[10] at that website and was informed by Susan Hanf, Rotary History Specialist, that not until 1950 was "Service Above Self" formally approved as one of two mottoes of Rotary. The other was "He profits most who serves best." In 1989 "Service Above Self" was designated as the principal motto. In 2004 "He profits most who serves best" was changed to "They profit most who serve best."

The wagon wheel emblem was adapted in different ways to serve as the Club's emblem from 1906-1912 when a geared wheel was adopted. The official emblem was authorized in 1924. The official emblem is a wheel with six spokes, 24 cogs and a keyway. [10]

Rotary International became the official name in 1922. It was approved as a part of the new constitution and by-laws adopted at that year's international convention.

In 1917 President Arch. C Klumph proposed that an endowment be set up "For the purpose of doing good in the world." In 1928 after the endowment fund had grown to more than $5,000 U.S. dollars it was renamed the Rotary Foundation and became a distinct entity within Rotary International.

The Four Way Test was officially adopted in 1943. More information on the Test is available in the 2009 August edition of "The Rotarian."

In any event, the concepts involved in the principal motto and in the Four Way Test seemed to be made incarnate in the early leadership of the Bowling Green Rotary Club. As Kevin Mays, the President of our Club in 2009-2010, would like to say, "These men became not only members of Rotary – they became Rotarians."

---

[1] *Architecture of Warren County Kentucky 1790-1940*
[2] B.G. scrapbook (Student Weekly) 2-6-1935
[3] Allen County Historical Society
[4] *Bittersweet* by Jonathan Jeffrey and Michael Dowell
[5] Courtesy of the Kentucky Library
[6] Patty Ennis Reid (Mrs. Charles Reid)
[7] The Bowling Green Presbyterian Church
[8] The Bowling Green Railroad Depot and Railroad Museum
[9] Bowling Green City Hall
[10] History of Rotary.Org
[11] Bowling Green Visitors Bureau
[12] Vicki Elrod (member First Baptist Church)
[17] The Depot and Railroad Museum
[18] The Medical Center at Bowling Green
[19] *An Album of Early Bowling Green, Kentucky Landmarks* by Irene Moss Sumpter

the 1930s

At the first meeting in January 1930, the Club was back to thinking about Mammoth Cave. The announcement was made of a dinner of the Mammoth Cave National Park Association to be held at the Brown Hotel in Louisville on January 17. Bowling Green's own Max Nahm was a charter member of the MCNPA, which was formed in 1924 and was a former president. Max Nahm frequently gave programs at the BG Rotary Club. At the February 19, 1930 meeting, it was announced that the Mammoth Cave National Park Bill had passed both the Kentucky State House of Representatives and the State Senate. The bill provided for using a part of the ad valorem tax to buy land for Mamoth Cave National Park so that the Federal Government would then take over the proposition.

The silver anniversary of Rotary International was celebrated in Washington D.C. Our own Marshall Love, Sr. installed two radios so that our Club might listen to the program on February 26, 1930. In attendance were senators, ambassadors and other distinguished men of government, some from afar. R.I. President Eugene Newsom was the principal speaker and Dr. J.L Harman gave a firsthand report to the local Club at the first meeting in March.

On March 20, 1930, the country was in the midst of the national tragedy called the "Great Depression," and almost every individual and institution either had or would have to make adjustments to this worldwide economic phenomenon. Rotary had already dismissed its song leader and pianist, and would reduce its dues from $5 per month to $4.50 in the near future. The ladies of the Presbyterian Church would correspondingly reduce the price of

The 1930s

the meals they served each week to the members by 10 cents per meal.

But for one night, Rotary and their wives and guests would put the mundane out of their minds and enter an enchanted world of make believe. And make believe it was on this night of March 20, 1930. The Old Armory's, (located at the SW corner of 10th & Chestnut), Denhardt Hall looked like anything but an Armory. It was decorated in the motif of a tropical garden. P.C. (Pete) Deemer was the Rotarian in charge of decorations. He enlisted the help of Mrs. Deemer (Bess) and many workers and set out to make the transformation.

"The Daily News" article recounts it this way. "The ceiling was hung with southern wild smilax, a twinning greenhouse vine of the lily family with bright green foliage and gray moss, which partially concealed hundreds of colored lights. Palmetto, pine trees and needle pines were eclectically placed around the floor and a pool surrounded by swamp plants with lilies in the center completed the setting. The walls of the hall were completely hidden by a trellis fence covered with vines and flowers." Dinner was served by the ladies of the Episcopal Church to 433 guests, 254 of whom were from out of town. Ironically, this event was called the Inter-City Meeting. After dinner there were speeches by Eugene Newsom, President of

> **Decorations Praised**
> The guests were loud in their praise of the elaborate manner in which the large Armory drill hall was decorated. The ceiling was hung with southern wild smilax and gray moss which partially concealed hundreds of colored lights. Palmetto, pine trees and needle pines about the floor and a pool banked with swamp plants and lillies in the center added greatly to the effect of the setting. A trellis fence covered with vines and flowers completely obscured the side walls of the hall. The bare back wall of the hall was made beautiful by the placing of a number of large cedars against the wall with a garden gate and flowering dogwood trees in the foreground.
> President Newsom left this morning for Fort Wayne, Ind. where he is to deliver an address tonight. The visit to the local club was the only visit he made in Kentucky. He is a resident of North Carolina

Rotary International and others. The excitement of having an R.I. President in Bowling Green as speaker at this event was apparently lost on no one. A "Musical Revue" was provided by students from Western Kentucky State Teachers College. After the dinner program, the tables were removed or rearranged and there was dancing until midnight – dancing to the music of the Southern Syncopators. "Daily News" captions were "Enchanting Dreamland Greets Rotes," and "Denhardt Hall turned into Tropical Garden," and the newspaper description was – "The greatest event in the history of the Bowling Green Rotary Club." By almost every standard for measuring such occasions, it reached new heights and the accolades no doubt would go to many people; but especially to Pete and Bess Deemer and the committees involved. A week later, Mrs. Deemer was honored by the Club for her help.

On March 26, 1930 about 20 of our members drove over to Scottsville for the purpose of helping to organize a Scottsville Rotary Club and in April of that year, the Board voted to send President P.C. Deemer to attend the R.I. Convention to be held in Chicago June 23-27. This was the silver anniversary of Rotary. In April, the officers for the new Rotary year were named: Sam Cristal was to be president; Emory Dent, vice president; Sam Cook, secretary; and Henry Bradley, treasurer.

After all the flurry of activity, the casualness of summer was welcome. The Club would have a barbeque at the Rotary/Boy Scout Camp on June 18, 1931. On July 23, 1931 two boats for the camp were ordered and the painting of the clubhouse was authorized. On August 4th the Club Council held its first meeting at Sam Cristal's home. The Club was still meeting at the Presbyterian Church. On August 20th Frank Ennis, who had been so instrumental as chair of the Boys Work Committee and specifically with the Rotary Camp when he was a member in the early years, was a guest of vice president Emory Dent. A week later the initiation fees of Bill Matthews and Charlie Manning were remitted. Bill Matthews came to our Club directly from the Franklin Club. This brings up an interesting point: Initiation fees, preparatory to membership. Apparently, this was the club's modus operandi for many years and at some point was discontinued. This may be something that the club will want to look at in the future.

The 1930s

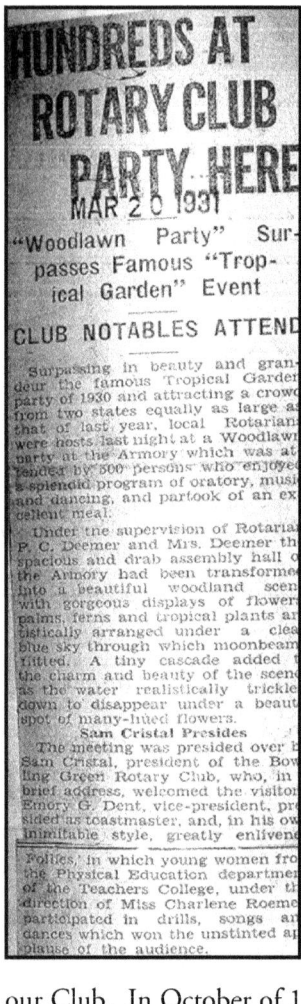

HUNDREDS AT ROTARY CLUB PARTY HERE
MAR 20 1931
"Woodlawn Party" Surpasses Famous "Tropical Garden" Event
CLUB NOTABLES ATTEND

On September 1, 1930, the publication of the "Pinion" was reinstituted after not being published for several years. We will see how long the publication of the "Pinion" lasts this time – I saw a publication called Rotoscript – one copy of which was published in 1931 and one in 1935. Stay tuned.

Rotarian Emory Dent agreed to mentor (look after) the Scottsville Club and to make periodic reports to our Club. In October of 1930, the doctors of Bowling Green agreed to run a free clinic for the county to check for physical defects of children. This of course continued the concern that the club has shown for children and honors the motto "Service Above Self." On November 26, 1930, Lon Causey's membership was reinstated.

On March 19, 1931, another great social extravaganza was held. Again it was held at the Armory. Members of the Club wondered if anything could approach the success of last year's event when the R.I. President was present. But, Pete Deemer and Mrs. Deemer were pros at this type of event. This time it was a "Woodlawn Party," and the drab Armory Hall (according to the

"Daily News") was transformed into a beautiful woodland scene with beautiful displays of flowers, palms, ferns and tropical plants artistically arranged under a clear blue sky through which moonbeams flitted. A tiny cascade added beauty to the many colored flowers. Sam Cristal, President of Rotary, presided and Emory Dent served as toastmaster. In his inimitable style, he greatly enlivened the proceedings. The group was entertained by "Forest Follies," a group of young women from the Physical Education Department of Western did drills, songs and dances which won unstinted applause from the audience. The feature of the program was an address by Rabbi, Joseph Rauch, of Temple Adath Israel in Louisville. Dr. Rauch lived up to his reputation as one of the leading orators in the United States. He touched upon Rotary as a factor in bringing about brotherly love as well as upon the hardships as a boy he experienced in Austria, his migration to the United States, his yearning for knowledge, and his struggle for an education. He made an eloquent plea for better understanding in the world and the great work being done by Rotary to bring that about. He held the rapt attention of the audience for 40 minutes. The dinner was served by the ladies of State Street Methodist Church. Music for dancing until an early hour of Friday morning was furnished by the Log Cabin Orchestra. When the evening came to a close, the event had surpassed the "Tropical Garden" extravaganza of last year with the attendance reaching 500. The Rotary Club, the wives and the guests had learned to celebrate that which is good and uplifting and to forget – at least temporarily – the troubling times.

The Club (Board) elected officers for 1931-32 at its April 29, 1931 meeting. James M. Hill was to be president and George H. Mosely was vice president. The Club kept Sam Cooke as secretary and Henry Bradley as treasurer. During this general period, Jimmy Hill reported on the programs for the Rotary/Boy Scout camp for the following year and Otis Clark asked for $125 to screen the dining room, and $150-175 to paint the lodge. Total cost was not to exceed $300.

On June 3, 1931, Dr. J.L. Harman, of the Business University, invited the Club to attend Commencement on June 4th at B.U. On July 6, 1931, it was announced that members' dues would be reduced by $1.00 per month and that a request would be made to the ladies of the Church to reduce the price of meals by 15 cents. The Club was dealing with the Depression. And, looking ahead, on July 8, 1931, Dr. A.M. Stickles, Head of the History Department at Western, addressed the Club on "Conditions in Germany." There would be many programs by Dr. Stickles in the coming years to try to enable the members of Rotary to understand the events preceding and during World War II in their historical context. At this same meeting Dr. James Blackburn, a local physician, was a guest. I asked our own Dr. John Blackburn (joined 6/9/1971) if they were related. The relationship was distant. The Club held a barbeque at the Camp on August 3, 1931. On August 12, 1931 a list of improvements to the Camp property were enumerated. The suggested improvements were to rock veneer the Clubhouse, to install a hydraulic ram to pump water to the Clubhouse, to build a cook's room or kitchen, to fix lounging areas, to clean trees (driftwood) out of the Creek, and to repair the access road. As you remember, the camp was located on Collett Road and Frank Collett (the road's namesake) was a guest on this day. On September 9, 1931, Dr. Hoy Newman was a guest. He was a physician and his office or rather the Newman Clinic was located in the block of East Main beyond the Helm on the corner of Main and Chestnut. A clinic at that time accepted inpatients as well as outpatients. There were other physicians offices in the same block, including a later member of the club, Dr. Eldon Stone. On the opposite corner of Main and Chestnut was the office of Dr. L.O. Toomey who later would have an interesting Rotary tenure.

The last three months of 1931 saw Dr. E.B. Rose named chair of the Committee for the Blind. Dr. Rose asked the members to help secure the names of the blind in Warren County. The Club then turned its attention to education. Rotarians were to mentor school children to improve their attendance. The Club was informed that every day one of four students was absent. The Club came up with the idea of giving a library of 40 books to the county school and to the city school that had the best attendance record for one year.

The father-son-daughter day Christmas get-together was to be December 23, 1931. Again this was the forerunner of the Christmas Party that Rotarians and their children and grandchildren enjoy today.

At the February 17, 1932 meeting Alonzo M. (Lon) Causey and Bill Richeson were appointed to the Airport Committee. Lon Causey was the father of L.D. Causey who served on the airport board for many years. Early in 1932, Rotarian J. Murray Hill, Sr. was promoted as a candidate for director of Rotary International. And on March 16, 1932, W.H. Mason was a guest of Jimmie Hill and introduced to the Club as such. W.H. Mason was the father of our own Billy Mason (joined Rotary April 3, 1986).

In March 1932, a dinner relating to an airport was held at the Helm and in May of that year Dr. John H. Blackburn addressed the Club. In June of 1932 the Club, in spite of hard times, paid the balance of its pledge – $1,000 – to the College Heights Foundation. Alex Downing would have been proud.

Significantly, selections were made for the Library Awards, discussed earlier, for the 1931-32 year for best attendance. On September 21, 1932 Pete Deemer reported that he had delivered the libraries to the winners – White's Chapel in the Boyce Community in the county and Ford Springs in the city. Ford Springs (aka Cool Springs School) was located behind the now non-existent High Street High School, which was located on State Street between Second and Short streets. The school was the first black primary school in the city and met in a residential type house, also serving as the custodians' house. It (Ford Springs School) set on an area bounded by Chestnut and Short Streets, which is now a warehouse area of Capital Window and Door Company.

The announcement about the libraries was followed by the notification that one of our charter members, Dr. L.O. Carson was resigning. Whereupon, the Board made Dr. Carson an honorary member. Honorary members pay only the price of the meal each time they attend. It is an honor given to members who have contributed to the life of Rotary in ways beyond those of the rank and file. There have been numerous honorary members over the almost 90 years of the life of the Club.

For those of us who attended Western State Teachers College, it is of note that Dr. Gordon Wilson, head of its English Department in the 1950s, and noted ornithologist, addressed the Club on October 12, 1932 on of all things – birds. Dr. Gordon Wilson was one of the all-time greatest college professors that I ever had. He knew a lot about genealogy and a lot more about each student's genealogy than the student himself or herself knew. Later Dr. Wilson's son, Gordon Wilson, Jr, was head of the Chemistry Department.

On November 16, 1932, the Club recognized one of our charter members, Dr. Ed Rose, a dentist. You will remember that Dr. Rose was the authorized organizer of our Club. On this day, he was recognized for having been appointed the Dean of the Dental College of the University of Tennessee located at Memphis, Tennessee – Local Boy does good. Also, on that day, U.S. Senator M.M. Logan addressed the Club. To start off December 1932, George Mosely announced that the drive for the Welfare Home, in which Rotary had long participated, was within $600.00 of reaching its goal of $7,500.00.

As the Christmas season approached, the Club was apprised of the upcoming meeting at which a Rotarians' sons and daughters would be invited. It was the Father-Son or Daughter Christmas Program; although, this year it was held on December 28, three days after Christmas. As we have previously indicated it was the forerunner of our present day Christmas party for the children and/or grandchildren of Rotarians. Closing out December, it was announced that the drive for the Welfare Home now lacked only $178.00 before it met its goal. They were still meeting at the Presbyterian Church, dues had been reduced from $5.00 to $4.50 and the ladies of the church have reduced the meal price from 60 cents to 50 cents.

On February 1,1933, Emory Dent presented Dr. G.Y. Graves as a new member. Later, his Co-founder Dr. J.T. Gilbert of the Graves-Gilbert Clinic would be a member of Rotary. The Graves-Gilbert Clinic was located on the west side of State Street between Eleventh and Twelfth Street. The building is still there and is now occupied by the Barren River District Health Department. The Graves-Gilbert Clinic is now a massive building located on Chestnut Street about a block from the By-Pass and is connected to the Medical Center by a pedway. Today most medical specialties are represented at the Clinic.

In late February 1933, T.T. Gardner, head of the Welfare Home Board told the Club that the Welfare Home is telling their recipients that their welfare would be cut next year if they did not plant a garden and that they would be checked by the Welfare Home. He also said that free seed potatoes would be distributed. Later, Victory Gardens would become very popular during World War II and still later, the City of Bowling Green would offer garden plots at Kereiakes Park to those who did not have a place in the back yard to accommodate a vegetable garden. There are still many of us, especially those with a rural background that are avid gardeners. In contemporary times, Dr. Nelson Rue (joined Rotary 1-31-1968), one of the surgeons at Graves-Gilbert Clinic, frequently brought tomato plants in the late spring and gave them to any Rotarian so desiring. Dr. Rue was one of those avid gardeners.

On March 22, 1933, J. R. Meany (later of Meany and Associates, Certified Public Accountants) addressed the Club on the city manager form of government. The motion was made by Emory Dent and seconded by A.M. Causey that the Club back this form of government. The seeds of the city manager form of government had been planted but it would be almost forty years before they would begin to grow and reach fruition. Chuck Coates (Joined Rotary in 1982) was the longest serving City Manager of Bowling Green and was a past President of this Club (1995-1996).

In July of 1933, W.L. Matthews was installed as President of Rotary. Bill Matthews was a Vice-President of the Business University from 1938-1963. He had previously served as Superintendent of schools at both Franklin and Livermore, Kentucky. He also had directed the Western Training School. He had served as a Director of the Kentucky Association of Independent Colleges. He was married to Miss Grace Thomas Voss. They had one daughter, Nancy M. Byran, who was a recorder at Western State College and one son, W.L. Matthews, Jr. who was Dean of the University of Kentucky College of Law from 1957-1971. The Bowling Green Business University was greatly enhanced by the presence of W.L. Matthews, Sr.[13]

On July 26, 1933, James R. Meany addressed the Club on the National Recovery Act, NRA (a New Deal Agency). About a month later, Mr. Max Nahm addressed the Club on the same subject. Max Nahm along with Dr.

A.M. Stickles was to become a regular guest lecturer in the years leading up to WWII and the war years themselves. Remember, earlier we talked about the Club trying to increase school attendance. Before the Club started its emphasis, on attendance, the average attendance was about 75%. A year later when the county school Whites Chapel won one of the libraries given by Rotary, the attendance was 96.08%. The club was addressed by the noted retailer, J.C.Penney. Mr. Penney was from White Plains, New York and spoke on the subject of "The Economic Situation Today".

On April 25, 1934 the Club elected officers. Those chosen were W.C. (Uncle Billy) Sumpter, President; C.M. (Clarence) Gaines, Vice-President. C.M. Gaines was the son of "Daily News" Founder John B. Gaines and Mr. Gaines was the father of Rotarians John B. Gaines and the grandfather of our own Pipes Gaines. C.M. Gaines was also the father of Rotarian Ray Gaines. As far as I can tell, Sam Cook was the first to be named both Secretary and Treasurer. Also, at the April 25,1934 meeting, Pete Deemer and Joe Garmon reported on a meeting in Nashville regarding Highway 31-W and of an intensive effort to establish a National Park in the Florida Everglades and central to this issue of the advantage of Bowling Green having a road from Chicago to the Everglades that would pass through Bowling Green. At the noon meeting on Oct 31,1934, President Sumpter complimented V.P. Clarence Gaines, publisher of the "Park City Daily News" (now the "Daily News") on publication of the souvenir edition on Mammoth Cave which advertised Bowling Green as the gateway to Mammoth Cave.

Ladies Night in 1934 was held at the Helm Hotel on November 20,1934. Clubs in the area were invited and J. Murray Hill, Sr. was the featured speaker. He and Mrs. Hill had just returned from Europe and Cairo, Egypt. Rotarian Hill was president of the Bowling Green Business University, director of two banks, and a past director of World Rotary. He was sent abroad (twice) to represent Rotary International. He was District Governor and President of our Club in 1940-1941. Besides visiting in Cairo, the Hills visited in England, France, Italy and Palestine. Rotarian Hill contrasted economic conditions in England and the U.S. The cost of the meal was 75 cents per plate and after the meal a dance followed.

The Rotary Hobby Fair was scheduled for May 1935.

On December 12,1934 the Club endorsed the formation of a Chamber of Commerce. On January 30, 1935 it was announced that the Highway 31-W banquet would be held at the Helm Hotel on the following Friday evening and it was also announced that the President's second annual ball for the benefit of children with infantile paralysis would be held on April 17, 1935. John B. Rodes spoke on the business recovery.

In June 1934, it was back to the Helm Hotel for our meetings. On April 4,1933 the following officers were elected:

President: L.T. Smith

Vice-President: James R. Meany

Directors: G.Y. Graves ,Douglas Willock and W.W. Holman

They would take office July 1,1935. On July 1,1935, Murray Hill spoke regarding the establishment of a south entrance to the Mammoth Cave National Park. It would be somewhere near Dripping Springs. This would be requested of the Mammoth Cave National Park Association.

On May 5,1934, Jimmie Hill discussed the Hobby Fair and Harry Spillman of New York City was the guest speaker.

On September 12,1934, George Mosely told of plans to dedicate the airport, and President Sumpter appointed: George Mosely, John Martin and Pete Deemer to the Airport Committee.

On September 26,1934 it was announced that the Crippled Children's Clinic would be held the next day at the Presbyterian Church, and on October 3,1934 the Club listened to the World Series game between the Detroit Tigers and the St. Louis Cardinals via radio. The secretary read a letter addressed to President Sumpter from Murray Hill written September 29, 1934 while on board a ship in the Adriatic Sea on his way to Cairo, Egypt on a mission for Rotary International.

At the meeting on September 11,1935 charter member and now Honorary member Dr. J.O. Carson was a guest as was Bill Craig, son of charter member, W.J. Craig. This would be a good place to relate a story about W.J. Craig. As you know he was a Western professor. In 1930, he built a large and beautiful home on Nashville Road a short distance from Normal Boulevard

The 1930s

(now University Boulevard). It had a spacious yard. At some point during his occupancy of this house, he planted a large display of yellow daffodils in the shape of the Rotary wheel. Many if not most, of you have observed this reminder of Rotary, as you have driven by this property in the early spring. Interestingly enough, after W.J. Craig's time, it became the property of the late Rotarian, Dr. Tom Baird and his wife Nancy (Tom joined Rotary 7/24/1963 and died in 2009 – one week after receiving his Rotary pin for 46 years of perfect attendance).[14] Later in 1935 (September 25th) the Club voted to purchase an American flag and a Rotary flag. These two flags have become an integral part of each meeting. It is something to wonder about as to what they used before these were purchased and I am sure that in the ensuing seventy five years that those flags have been replaced numerous times –the honor remains the same-ask Colonel Spiller.

On November 20, 1935, the initiation fee for new members was reduced from $20 to $10. Again, the depression was taking its toll in various ways and with many people who did not always make the news. But in December of 1935, it was announced that the Bowling Green Christmas Parade would be held on December 14th. It was to be under the auspices of the

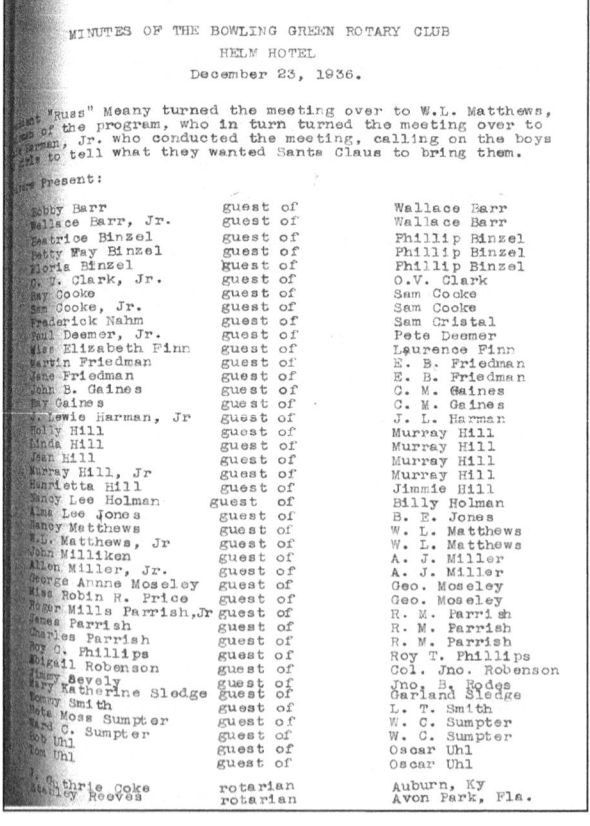

Chamber of Commerce and the "Park City Daily News" (later to be just the "Daily News"). The parade was to be 1 ½ miles long and was to feature live reindeer. On December 11,1935 Top Orendorf was introduced as a new member. He was to be one of the giants in Rotary and in the community. He, among other things, was President of the Club 1939-1940, was master of ceremonies at the 50th anniversary dinner in 1970 and was the after dinner speaker at the 75th anniversary dinner in 1995.

At the December 18th meeting, the Club decided to meet on December 23rd for its regular meeting instead of Christmas day (such dedication, that they would even consider meeting on Christmas Day). At the December 23rd meeting, President L.T. Smith advised the Club that past President of R.I. would be in Bowling Green to give the commencement address at the Business University on May 26, 1936 and that the Club should try to get him to address the Inter-city meeting the next evening May 27, 1936. Let me go back to November 27th. Dr. A.M. Stickles, head of the History Department at Western State Teachers College, addressed the club on the "Foreign Situa-

> "Abdication and Ascension" was the subject of an address by Dr. A. M. Stickles of the Western Kentucky State College at today's meeting of the Rotary Club at the Helm Hotel. In the opinion of the speaker, desire of former King Edward VIII to wed Mrs. Simpson was not the sole reason for the abdication.
>
> "Evidence of friction in England has been apparent sinve the abcendancy of Edward VIII," the speaker declared. "Reading between the lines it is apparent that Edward wished to govern and not merely reign. His desire to remedy conditions among the coal miners of Wales and the people of London's slums caused a friction between the Crown and Parliament comparable to an attempt to increase taxation, thereby cutting into the profits of the big business interests of England."
>
> In the speaker's opinion Edward VIII was dissatisfied with the French Alliance and probably preferred closer relationship with Germany.
>
> "As a man Edward VIII did right in abdicating, but as a King he made 'a mess of it' to use the language of the street," Dr. Stickles added.

Narrative of this event is found on pages 38, 39 and 40.

tion". The storm clouds of what would become World War II were beginning to form as thunderheads on the distant horizon.

At the first meeting in January of 1936 Russ (J.R.) Meany addressed the club on the "Social Security Act". The Christmas program for the Rotarians, sons or daughters got pushed forward to January 15th. Looking over the list of progeny attending, one can see the "Juniors" and others that would be in the coming years the leaders in Rotary and the community.

Noted Sociologist And Lecturer To Be Speaker Tomorrow Evening

Dr. Allen D. Albert, noted sociologist and lecturer of Paris, Ill., is to address a public meeting at the First Baptist church tomorrow evening at 7:45 o'clock.

The speaker is being brought to Bowling Green by the local Rotary club as the first of four noted lecturers to appear here over a four-week period in an "Institute of International Understanding" sponsored by the club.

The purpose of the institute is "to increase the understanding by the people of one country of the problems of other countries and the thinking of their peoples."

"Better understanding of others' problems and thoughts," the sponsors believe, "will lead to good will which must exist if there is to be international peace."

Other speakers in the series will appear here October 27 and November 3 and 10. Those programs will be held in Snell Hall auditorium on the Western Teachers College campus.

Dr. Albert, according to a release from the Chicago office of Rotary International, has had an interesting career as a newspaper man, having begun as a reporter in Washington, D. C., and New York. He was a war correspondent in the Spanish-American war, Chief Editorial Writer for the Washington, D. C., Times from 1895-1910, Publisher of the Columbus (Ohio) News from 1910-1911, and Editor and Associate Publisher of the Minneapolis Tribune from 1912-1916.

As assistant to the president for the Chicago Century of Progress, it was his responsibility to visit many of the European capitals on diplomatic missions relative to the exposition, and also to be commissioner of the exposition to Japan and China.

For a number of years Dr. Albert has been especially interested in the causes of city growth and programs of city development, having been consultant to many city development bodies. He is a member of the American Academy of Political and ——————— and was special lec-

Dr. Allen D. Albert

and Political Science in the University of Minnesota from 1912-1913. He received the degree Sc.D. in sociology from Evansville College in 1922.

He is the author of many articles on city planning, city analysis, and social changes. He is also the author of articles in encyclopedias on "World Fair Architecture."

Dr. Albert has been very active in the Rotary club movement, having served as President of Rotary International, and as a Rotary speaker on many occasions. He has delivered anniversary addresses for the Rotary clubs of Chicago, New York, Boston, Minneapolis, Omaha, and other cities. He made the opening address at the Institute of International Relations for two years at Nashville, Tenn., spoke at the Institute of International Affairs at the Southern Methodist University at Dallas, Texas, and during 1937-1938 addressed one hundred and fourteen Institutes of International Understanding, sponsored by individual

On January 22,1936, Rotary pledged $565.00 to the Welfare Home drive. This was more than any other civic club. On February 17th, 1936 the Club endorsed the candidacy of Will R. Manier of the Nashville Club for Rotary International President, on February 5th, 1936, Rotarian, Top Orendorf, addressed the Club on " The New King of England". You will remember the great international saga of Edward VIII. Edward was the oldest son of King George V and

DR. ALLEN ALBERT HEARD BY 350 AT MEETING TUESDAY

Armory Beautifully Decorated For State Meeting Here

Dr. Allen D. Albert, Chicago, past president of Rotary International, addressed about 350 Kentucky Rotarians and their guests at a state meeting last night at the local Armory on the subject, "International Spread of Rotary."

Dr. Albert was introduced by Will R. Manier, Nashville attorney slated for the next presidency of Rotary International.

John Allen Lewis, famous radio baritone who formerly resided in Bowling Gren, was unable to appear on the program because of illness, and in his absence, three numbers were sung by Joseph McPherson of radio station WSM, Nashville.

Mr. Lewis is reported to have been bitten by a mad dog several days ago at Nashville, and is now undergoing treatment.

The Deemer Floral Company converted the large auditorium of the armory into a beautiful "outdoor garden" through the generous use of wild huckelberry vines from Georgia, wisteria, Oregon huckleberry and thousands of cut and potted flowers.

The outdoor effect was heightened by placing of the flags of the 40 nations in which Rotary Clubs are organized along the edge of the balcony of the room. These flags were waving in a "breeze" which came from a number of concealed electric fans. An indirect lighting effect added to the beauty of the room.

Queen Mary. He became King on January 20, 1936. Edward fell in love with the American divorcee, Wallis Warfield Simpson. Because his government was opposed to accepting her as Queen, Edward abdicated his throne on December 11, 1936. His brother, George VI, who succeeded him, gave him the title of Duke of Windsor. The Duke and Mrs. Simpson were married in June of 1937 in France. Edward left England in self-imposed exile. George VI served dur-

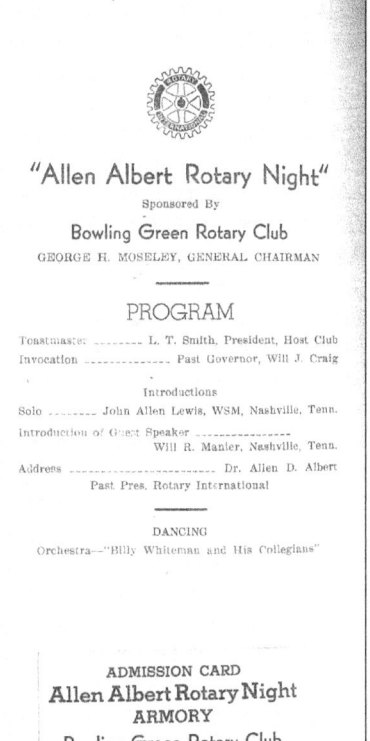

"Allen Albert Rotary Night"
Sponsored By
Bowling Green Rotary Club
GEORGE H. MOSELEY, GENERAL CHAIRMAN

PROGRAM

Toastmaster .... L. T. Smith, President, Host Club
Invocation .... Past Governor, Will J. Craig
Introductions
Solo .... John Allen Lewis, WSM, Nashville, Tenn.
Introduction of Guest Speaker ....
.... Will R. Manier, Nashville, Tenn.
Address .... Dr. Allen D. Albert
Past Pres. Rotary International

DANCING
Orchestra—"Billy Whiteman and His Collegians"

ADMISSION CARD
Allen Albert Rotary Night
ARMORY
Bowling Green Rotary Club

ing one of the most troubled periods in Great Britain's history. He was very popular because of his untiring devotion to royal duty. During World War II, King George VI and the royal family endeared themselves to the British people by sharing in the hardships and dangers – including the bombing of London,etc. During his reign India became an independent country (1947). King George VI was succeeded by his oldest daughter, (age 25) Queen Elizabeth II, upon his death on February 6, 1952. Queen Elizabeth II still reigns.

On March 11,1936, George Moseley, chair of the Inter-city meeting announced that the event would be held on May 26,1936. Allen Albert, past President of R. I. was to be the speaker. The following assignments were made by President of the Club, L.T. Smith: George Mosely, Chairman, Emory Dent –Meeting Hall, W.J. Craig Sr. – Reception, J. Murray Hill, Sr. – securing the speaker, Jimmie Hill-dinner dance, Robinson and Schmid-Parking, Scout Master Bannet – Boy Scouts, W.L. Matthews, Sr. –Publicity invitations, P.C. (Pete) Deemer –Decorations.

On March 18, 1936 John B. Rodes was elected to membership. Rotarian Rodes had been Mayor of Bowling Green from 1929-1933. He later would be Circuit Judge. Doug Willock was reinstated as a member, classification public attorney behind John B. Rodes, and President L.T. Smith was selected to attend the R.I. Convention in Atlantic City June 22-26.

On May 26,1936, Allen Albert night was celebrated in conjunction with the Inter-city meeting. Dr. Allen Albert of Chicago was a past President of Rotary International. The event was held at Denhardt Hall in the local Armory at 10th and Chestnut Streets. According to the "Park City Daily News" (now the "Daily News") the large audito-

Photo from Kentucky Library collection.

The 1930s

Photo from Kentucky Library collection.

rium of the Armory was transformed into a beautiful outdoor garden through the generous use of wild huckleberry vines from Georgia, Wisteria, Oregon huckleberry and thousands of cut and potted flowers. The outdoor effect was heightened by the placing of 40 flags representing the 40 nations that then had Rotary Clubs. The flags were placed around the edge of the balcony of the hall. These flags were waving in a breeze generated by concealed electric fans. An indirect lighting effect added to the beauty and the ambience of the setting. All of this was accomplished by a committee chaired by P.C. (Pete) Deemer, owner of Deemer Floral Company. There were about 350 Rotarians and guests present to hear Dr. Albert talk about "The International Spread of Rotary". Dr. Albert was introduced by President elect of R.I. Will Manier of the Nashville Rotary Club. Bowling Green Rotarians, as well as, regional Rotarians must have wondered "how much better does it get than having two R.I. Presidents in Bowling Green at the same time".

Photo from Kentucky Library collection.

At the meeting on June 24,1936, conditions of Drakes Creek at the Rotary camp were discussed, specifically, the accumulation of trees, logs and driftwood. These could be an endangerment to swimmers. This apparently had been something that had been going on for some time and had continued to worsen. No action was taken at this meeting but it is something that would eventually lead to drastic corrective

Rotary Club Honors Sam Cristal As Charter Member

Sam Cristal, 83, one of the few remaining charter members of the local Rotary club, formed in 1921, was recently made an honorary member of that organization.

The oldest known living graduate of the Bowling Green Business university, Mr. Cristal came to Bowling Green to enter the business school in 1882 from Memphis. He was graduated from the institution in 1886 and his diploma now hangs in the school library.

Mr. Cristal came to America from Odessa, Russia, on the Black sea, and moved here shortly after crossing the ocean. After finishing school he accepted a bookeeping position with Nahm Brothers dry good store here. Mr. Cristal said he was so happy with his first job that he memorized every account on the ledger and learned the customers by sight and remembered the number of the page on which their account appeared.

Mr. Cristal later became a member of Sam Nahm and Company firm and remained active in the business until a short time ago.

He married Miss Hattie Nahm, a daughter of Sam Nahm, in 1892. He has two sons, Phillip, who is connected with the Northwestern Life Insurance company in Milwaukee, and Charles, who is an executive with the Cleveland Electrical Construction Company.

Mr. Cristal was active in many civic organizations until his health failed a few months ago. He played

Sam Cristal

a vital part in obtaining the Bowling Green City hospital and was a member of the first board of directors for that institution.

He later became active in crippled children's work throughout Kentucky. Mr. Cristal was a member of the Kentucky Cripple Children's board for three years and played a vital part in gaining many new services for the unfortunate children. He was director of the Bowling Green Chamber of Commerce in

(Continued on Page 14, Column 4)

Rotary Club Honors Sam Cristal

—(Continued from Page 7)

1937.

Several years ago a Sam Cristal Day was proclaimed by the members of the Rotary club in his honor. At that meeting a letter of commendation for his work was given him from each member of the club.

One of the Rotarians recently stated that: "Mr. Cristal is regarded by his fellow Rotarians as probably being the best man in Bowling Green."

During the first World War one of the study clubs of Bowling Green was meeting, with Mr. Cristal as a guest. The subject was Palestine. At the time much was being said about the "Back to Jerusalem" movement.

When Mr. Cristal was invited to participate in the discussion, a member asked: "Mr. Cristal do you want to return to Jerusalem?"

"No," he replied positively. "I for ly Jerusalem when I came to America as a poor boy and you took me in and gave me a chance to work and be happy. No, I don't want my bones to go to Jerusalem, I want to be buried in Fairview cemetery with my friends rather than taken to Louisville and buried among Jews whom I never knew."

Members of the club rated that statement as one of the most patriotic made during the war.

Mr. Cristal resides at his home at 618 East Main street and for the past several months his health has been poor.

Unemployment A

action. Turning to other things, it was announced that another crippled children's clinic would be held at the Presbyterian Church on Tuesday, July 14th. On July 22, 1936, Secretary Cooke read a letter from Will R. (Bill) Manier of Nashville thanking the Club for the telegram sent to him in Atlantic City, congratulating him on his election to the Presidency of R.I. Remember, our local Club was one of his earliest supporters in his race for R.I. President.

On August 26, 1936, Dr. Ed Rose, charter member and organizer of this club, was a guest of Dr. E. Wallace Barr. Dr. Rose was now Dean of the University of Tennessee Dental School at Memphis. About a month later, Dr. J. O. Carson, a charter member and the person who furnished the inspiration to establish the Crippled Children's Committee, was a guest of the Club. Dr. Carson was now an honorary member of this club and on Feb. 3, 1937, James R. Meany addressed the Club on unemployment compensation, old age benefits and social security — all New Deal Programs. On April 7, 1937 the whole Club roster was nominated for Director. When the votes were counted two weeks later the winners were George Mosely, J. Murray Hill, Sr., A.J. Miller, Top Orendorf and Douglas Willock. Others elected that should be mentioned were W.L. (Bill) Matthews was elected District Governor

CLUB APPROVES EXTENSION OF CEMETERY PIKE

Resolution Passed Okehing Road Project

A resolution to support the movement for an extension of the road known as Cemetery pike from Cassaday's store to Meador and Settle was adopted at the regular noon meeting of the Rotary Club today at the Helm hotel.

The motion was offered by L. B. Finn after a report of the findings of a committee composed of J. L. Harman and M. C. Ford, recently named to investigate the road situation. Mr. Finn's motion also included authority to interest other civic bodies in the project and ask the Warren fiscal court for work on the road.

It was pointed out at the meeting that the new Smiths Grove-Scottsville road, now under construction, would mean the transfer of considerable farm trade from Bowling Green to Scottsville unless improvements are completed on the road leading to Meador and Settle.

The program at the meeting today consisted of vocal solos by B. F. Austin of Morganfield, who was accompanied by Miss Elizabeth Taylor of Owensboro.

Visitors at the meeting were Rotarian Byron Burns of Cincinnati, Dr. William Douglas of Brewton, Ala., Clifton Bradley of Louisville, Roger Smith of Louisville, and E. H. Binzel, Russell Miller and F. H. Moore, all of this city.

Rotarians Donate To Camp KYSOC

The Bowling Green Rotary Club yesterday voted to donate $600 to help construct an administration building at Camp KYSOC, an especially designed camp for physically handicapped children of Kentucky.

The local club's donation was for the 1959-60 year and is expected to be duplicated during the present fiscal year.

Rotary clubs throughout Kentucky are joining in an effort to raise $70,000 or construction of the camp's administration building. The local club made its contribution after the project had been explained by Dr. L. O. Toomey, Rotarian and a leader in this ea of the effort to raise funds the camp.

amp KYSOC is being constructed under auspices of the entucky Society for Crippled Children. It will be situated on a 124-acre site in an undeveloped area that formerly was a part of Butler State Park, near Carrollton.

In addressing the club, Charles Collins, director of the War Memorial Boys' Club, emphasized the need for moving the local Boys' Club to a proposed new location near the 11th Street Fire Station.

Collins pictured the present location as entirely unsuitable, at the Lexington District Conference and Bill Matthews was chosen by our Club as a delegate to the R. I. Convention to be held in Nice, France in June. J. Murray Hill was elected as alternate. On May 26th our thoughts again turned to the Rotary camp and the ongoing problems regarding the logs obstructing the normal flow of the creek. A couple of months later a committee comprised of Bill Matthews, Pete Deemer, Garland Sledge, L.T. Smith and Bill Holman were appointed to investigate selling the property.

On August 4,1937 a resolutions committee was named to draw up resolutions lamenting the death of Western Kentucky State Teachers College and former President of the Bowling Green Rotary Club, Dr. H.H. Cherry. The committee was composed of Dr. J.L. Harman, Sr., John B. Rodes and charter member Sam Cristal. Three weeks later, Dr. J. L. Harman read these resolutions at the noon meeting. Earlier, in August, J. Murray Hill, Sr. addressed the Club on his recent trip to the R.I. Convention in Nice, France, and the assembly in Switzerland. At that September 1,1937 meeting. Dr. J.L. Harman outlined the plan for raising the money to complete the statue of Dr. H. H. Cherry which stands as a landmark in front of Cherry Hall. Speaking of Cherry Hall, let us go back to the laying of the cornerstone of Cherry Hall at a ceremony on October 27,1936.[5] There is a document called "The Laying of the Cornerstone"[15] which is included in "The Documents" section of this treatise. There were some speakers during the fall of 1937 that were well known then or would become well known names in the near future. They were Reverend Gypsy Smith, Jr. noted evangelist, Barry Bingham, Sr., publisher of the "Louisville Courier-Journal" and the "Louisville Times" and Judge Mac Swinford who would hold court many times as Federal Judge in our federal building located on Main and Center Streets many times. Bill Thompson addressed the Club in his capacity as Secretary of the Mammoth Cave National Park Association, and Dr. Stickles addressed the Club again on the foreign situation.

Sam Cristal Day was held on December 22,1937. John B. Rodes spoke on Sam Cristal – the man, Rotarian Ford on his ethical ideals, Dr. J.L. Harman, Sr. on his Rotary activities and Lawrence Finn on his community contributions. Remember, Sam Cristal was a charter member; his classification was produce, and he was with the Sam Nahm Company located at 823 State Street –less than a block north of the square.

On March 16, 1938 Roland Fitch, Sr. was introduced as a new member. Also, at that meeting, the Club endorsed the drive for funds by the Kentucky Crippled Children's Committee starting Easter Sunday. This was the origin of the Easter Seal Campaign and the portender of Camp Kysoc. On April 16, 1938, L.T. Smith, Murray Hill and Paul L. Garrett were appointed to a committee to report to the Club on "The Equality of Women Proposition". Charter night at Horse Cave was to be April 29, 1938. The new officers for the following year were to be: Douglas Willock, President and to help him were to be: Top Orendorf, J. Murray Hill, Sr., W.L. Roemer and J.L. Thurber. Bill Matthews would be our delegate to the R.I. Convention in San Francisco.

In June of 1938, the Club discussed the conditions of Cemetery Pike, and in August of 1938 the Club endorsed the extension of Cemetery Pike from Cassiday's Store to Meador and Settle (See "Park City Daily News") article dated 08/31/1938), which is in the Document Section.

For the second time a Christmas Party for the children of Rotarians in 1938. This and the 1936 program were much like our present Christmas parties and would be about as close to a prototype of an origin as we could find.

Nostalgically, in October 1938, the Club decided to sell the Rotary-Boy Scout Camp on Drakes Creek. Each Board member signed the deed to the Rotary camp sale on May 10, 1938. The logs and driftwood had won out. It had been a fixture of Rotary from the very earliest. There were many happy times associated with it and it had meant a lot to the Boy Scouts. The year of 1938 concluded with one of Dr. Stickles programs entitled "The Jewish Situation".

The Club wasted no time in securing another piece of property for a Boy Scout Camp. This one was located on Plum Springs Road near Barren River. It was a 45-acre tract known as the Ed Hudgens tract. It was on the north side of the river and was equidistant from Louisville Road and Richardsville Road. It included an 8-acre island connected by a slough. It was good for sea scouts (older boys). It had an old log house on the property which could be remodeled for a headquarters. It was on the north side of the river but very close to

The 1930s

Beech Bend. The motion to buy the property was made by George Mosely and seconded by W.J. Craig. The purchase price was $1,100. The Club would pay $600 down and the balance $125 a year until paid. Motion to buy this property was made on April 26, 1939.

On May 26, 1937 the Club voted to buy repair materials and enlist the help of the WPA to do the work. Cost was not to exceed $29. On May 31, 1939, M.C. Ford addressed the Club on "Dictators of the World", and on November 22, 1939 Dr. Stickles spoke on "The European Situation".

On July 12, 1939 the Club authorized spending $75 to fix up a mess hall and kitchen at the Old Barn at the new camp site. Earlier in July, Max Nahm spoke to the Club on "What Happens to $100 Deposited in a Bank". And on September 6, the Club voted to sponsor an international institute. Marty Garvin Deputy, would have been proud. Marty's brother, David Garvin, was later a member of this club.

---

[1] Architecture of Warren County, Kentucky 1790-1940
[4] *Bittersweet* by Jonathan Jeffrey and Michael Dowell
[5] Kentucky Library and Museum
[6] Patty Ennis Reid (Mrs. Charles Reid)
[12] Vicki Elrod (member of First Baptist Church)
[13] The *Daily News*
[14] Nancy Baird (Kentucky Library)
[15] Kentucky State Highway Department District #3

the 1940s

The 1940's were the war years and the impact on the Club was seen in many ways, but most importantly, it was seen in the way that the Club responded — the true patriotism that was engendered. It showed up in the programs. So many of the programs were about the war and I believe that the Club was involved in at least 8 War Bond Drives some of which were held after the war ended and were called victory drives. To start off the decade, Top Orendorf was our President to be followed by J.Murray Hill, Sr. and then President Paul L. Garrett, President of Western Kentucky State Teachers College, was President when Pearl Harbor occurred. In early January 1940, the invitation was made (probably at the suggestion of Emory Dent) that the State Highway Dept. move its district office to Bowling Green.[16] That office has been a part of the Bowling Green community all these years and is presently located on Morgantown Road. On January 24,1930 Club members asked the W.P.A. to remove the driftwood on the 8 acre island at the new camp and the Club asked that the wood be given to the poor. Almost three years later in December of 1942, President Roosevelt ordered that the W.P.A. be dismantled. Emory Dent reported on the work on the Louisville Pike 31-W North, on the Nashville Pike 31-W South and the Morgantown Road. On March 27,1940 Bowling Green's own Duncan Hines spoke to the Club on his book, "Adventures in Good Eating" published in 1936. And on April 10,1940, discussions were held as to whether to try to secure a CCC camp for Warren County. Also in April, officers were elected to serve during the Rotary year beginning July 1st. The new President was J. Murray Hill, Sr. and the Vice President was Paul L. Garrett. Directors were Pete Deemer, Fred Spires and C.H. Jaggers.

The Secretary/Treasurer continued to be Sam Cooke. On July 10, 1940, Dr. Stickles spoke on the subject "Will England Win the Last Battle". C.M. Gaines presented his son, John B. Gaines (father of Rotarian Pipes Gaines) as a new member and L.T. Smith presented Dr. H.L. Stephens, Western Kentucky State Teachers College, as a new member. Dr. Stephens would later become head of the Biology Department.

President Paul L. Garrett of WKSTC apprized the Club of "Boys State" which is to be held at Western. Rotary will sponsor a boy from Warren County.

On August 21, 1940, members of the Bowling Green Barons Baseball Team were guests of Rotary. Mike Powers was Manager and Vic Smith was President of the team. Local businessman Rick Kelley, who was most responsible for bringing the new state of the art baseball facility to this city in 2009 and the team "The HotRods" would no doubt have been inspired. Rick Kelley is the son of the late Rotarian, Tom Kelley, who was a member of the club for many years (Tom joined Rotary in 1964). Later in the summer, Lt. Governor Rodes K. Myers again addressed the Club, this time on national defense and local cooperation. On September 25, 1940 Rotary sponsored yet another Crippled Children's Clinic at the Presbyterian Church. On October 16, 1940, Rotarian, Ray Hopper, County Agent, took 2 local youths to Harrisburg, Pennsylvania to participate in a national dairy show. Warren County's dairy team won the national competition. The Rotary Club sent a telegram to Ray and the boys. And on October 30, 1940, Dr. A.M. Stickles again reminded the Club of what was going on in the world with an address entitled "The World Crisis".

In November of 1940, our own peripatetic Emory Dent, Highway Commissioner of the State of Kentucky, proposed the idea of rerouting 31-W through the city by building a 31-W Bypass. It followed what was then Laurel Avenue. It was completed in 1945. Four years later the new State Street Bridge was completed and was named the Emory G. Dent Bridge. In 1949, our Rotary Club undertook the lighting of the bridge. This tied in with the By-pass and is still a functional bridge across the river in 2009. After the Dent Bridge, there was not to be another bridge built across the river until

1987 when a new span was realized west of the Dent Bridge to connect with Highway 68-80 through the city.

In 1940 a custom of this Club that developed had a club member speak for 3 minutes on the business or profession of another Club member. First was Roland Fitch who spoke about James M. Hill's business. The H.A. McElroy Company had 17 stores, and Mr. Hill was the general manager.

In March of 1941, the Club revisited the idea of encouraging the city of Bowling Green to adopt a City Manager form of government and a committee was established to take this on. The committee consisted of Top Orendorf, Roland Willock and L.B. Finn. The Bowling Green City Hall located at College Street and 10th Avenue[1] was designed by Louisville architect Brinton B. Davis. It was built in 1907. Before this, the City Council met at 1019 State Street, a building that also had housed the volunteer Fire Department. After the establishment of a city Fire Department, the building was turned over to the City Police Department. The building now houses professional offices. The building experienced a fire in 1911. At some point, it was restored to its pre-1940 appearance. There is also some evidence that the City Council may have met in the building on the southeast corner of State and 10th Avenue before occupying City Hall. Brinton B. Davis later designed numerous buildings at Western Kentucky State College. Rotarian Frank Ennis did the concrete work on City Hall.

Later in July, H. Barkus Gray, Principal of Bowling Green High School, addressed the Club. Several Club members attended high school at BGHS on Center street. The next month Hubert Cherry moved and Henry Baird seconded that the Club send out letters requesting the views of the membership on the purchase of land for an airport. On December 24, 1941, the father-son and daughter Christmas meeting was held.

Christmas 1941 would have been a time of many reflections and many apprehensions about the immediate future, since it came less than 3 weeks after the Japanese attack on Pearl Harbor on December 7th, 1941. The Japanese Vice-Admiral led a 33-ship strike force within 200 miles (under cover of darkness) north of Oahu. His carriers launched about 360 planes against the Pacific fleet under the command of U.S. Admiral Kimmell and the Hawaiian ground troops under Lt. General Walter C. Short.

The first bombs fell at 7:55 AM and the chief targets were the eight American battle ships among the 92 naval vessels anchored in the harbor. The U.S. had 18 ships sunk or severely damaged, about 170 planes destroyed and suffered 3,700 casualties. "Remember Pearl Harbor" became a rallying cry for the United States during World War II. On December 8th, President Roosevelt asked Congress for a Declaration of War against Japan and through a joint resolution the Congress unhesitatingly responded in the affirmative that day. At 4:55 PM President Roosevelt approved the joint resolution and the country was officially at war. On December 11, Germany and Italy declared war on the United States and then Congress declared war on Germany and Italy.

Even though almost every program during the war years related, in some way, to the war, it is still amazing how Rotary kept on with the projects that they had been involved with, some for many years. In March of 1942, Everett Moore addressed the Club on the Derby Underwear manufacturing plant located on Church Street. The Derby was one of Bowling Green's earliest and most stable industries and was a major employer of women. It was a fixture in Bowling Green during the war years and beyond. Later, Fruit of the Loom, its parent company moved its corporate headquarters to the city and built a big new headquarters building on Fruit of the Loom Drive off of Lovers Lane. In March of 1941, again the entire Club was nominated for Director and later that month, Dr. A.M. Stickles addressed the Club on "The Situation in the Pacific". In April the members of the Club were furnished a respite by Coach E.A. Diddle. Western Kentucky's legendary basketball coach brought ten members of his 1940-1941 team to be guests of Rotary. The team had been runner-up in the N.I.T. Some of the members of that team were Dero Downing, later Principal of the training school and still later President of Western. He was one of Western's most beloved Presidents and there was absolutely no doubt that he loved Western equally as much. Still later, after his Presidency, he became head of the College Heights Foundation. That is now under the direction of his son, Rotarian Alex Downing. Also, on that team were Oran McKinney, Don Ray and Buck Sydnor.

At the start of the new Rotary year in early July 1942, the Club voted to sell the Rotary/Boy Scout camp located off Plum Springs Road on Barren River due to the lack of good drinking water, suitable water for swimming and suitable water for boating. The life of this camp was short compared to the one on Drakes Creek and so were the memories.

On August 19,1942, the Club embarked upon its first drive to collect scrap iron and about a month later the Board voted to buy another $1,000 war bond since it had $1,247.37 in the treasury – what generosity-what faith. On September 2, 1942, Dr. Harman announced that Sgt. York would be in Bowling Green on September 7, 1942. Later, in the year in November, a young man named Harold Logsdon, who was at Pearl Harbor on December 7,1941 when the attack occurred, addressed the Club and a couple weeks later, Dr. Stickles gave another one of his programs entitled "The North African Campaign." Remember the North African Campaign was brilliantly led by Field Marshall Montgomery. The British fought a see-saw battle for some time against the Germans and Italians. In May 1942, the great German general Rommel's African Corp. began a powerful offensive. They captured Tobruk in Libya and were moving toward Egypt. By July, strong British resistance and Rommel's supply shortage had halted the Axis attacks at El Alamein, Egypt. In October, the British eighth army under Montgomery took the offensive and rolled on to Tripoli and southern Tunisia. On November 8, 1942, U.S. General Dwight D. Eisenhower commanded a force that landed on the coast of Algeria and Morocco. About 500 troops and supply ships transported troops from the U.S. and the British Isles. The invasion caught the Germans by surprise. On May 12,1942 the last Axis Army force in Africa surrendered. The Allies had killed, wounded or captured 350,000 Axis soldiers. It was one of the turning points in the war.

On November 16,1942, Lewie Harman, Jr. , son of the legendary Rotarian, Dr. J.L. Harman, Sr. was home on furlough and was a special guest of the Club and on December 23rd, 1942 two other members of the Club now in service were guests. They were Phillip Brunson and Dr. J.T. Gilbert. Today (March 17,1943) was a sad day for the Club as the death of charter member Dr. J.O. Carson was reported. He had been one of the giants in the early days. A motion was made by W.J. Craig and seconded by Emory Dent that a resolution be prepared to commemorate him. The War Bond Sales Committee presented the program on April 14, 1943. George Mosely was the Chair of that committee. Amazingly, in just 12 minutes, the Club bought or pledged $87,125. in War bonds and in September 1943, the Club voted to sell $153,000. worth of bonds. In all of 1943, the Club either bought or sold $524,267.75 in War Bonds. The passion and commitment is as astounding today as it was 65 years ago and the patriotism is as touching. Many war bond drives were held in Fountain Square Park. If a citizen bought a bond, he or she received a free ride in an army jeep driven by an active duty soldier who was present just for that purpose.

Fountain Square Park[1] has been the focus of downtown Bowling Green since 1798 when Robert Moore donated the original 2 acre tract to the county for public use. In 1812 the state legislature incorporated the city of Bowling Green. There was originally a log courthouse that set in the area of what is now Fountain Square Park. By 1812 it had been replaced by a two story brick building. During the 1820's the Barren River was opened to steam navigation, and in 1859 the L & N Railroad was completed to Bowling Green.[17] In addition to the Court House, the town square was home to the town jail and a market house. Main Street being the most direct route to both the depot and the boat landing was a natural location for business development. The original brick courthouse on the square was abandoned upon completion of a new courthouse on East 10th Avenue between College and State Streets in 1869. This was on a part of a three acre tract of land owned by pioneer James Rumsey Skiles and had been the downtown terminal of the portage railroad. The present park was built between 1871 and 1872 according to the plans of John Cox Underwood who was both engineer of public works and Mayor and later Lt. Governor. The original stone fountain was replaced in 1881 by the present cast iron fountain. Statues of

the four seasons, benches and urns were all cast by J.W. Fiske of New York City. The stone arches were manufactured by the Smallhouse Marble Works in 1916, but the concept of a landscaped public park has retained much of the same appearance as when designed by John Cox Underwood in 1871.

In the middle of the year the Club voted to return to the Presbyterian Church for its meetings and meals.

Back to the war, When a member went into military services, his badge was put into a badge case decorated with red, white and blue ribbons and he was guaranteed Club membership when the war was over with the same classification.

In December 1943, President Jake Barnard announced two drives: one to raise funds for combating polio and one to raise funds for servicemen canteens. Again, the polio drive portended the massive drive that R.I. and all the local clubs, including the Bowling Green Rotary Club would be involved in called Polio-Plus which was instituted in the 1990's and continues in the first decade of the 21st Century.

On April 29, 1944 the Club honored Sam Cristal. Sam was 83 years old and was a charter member of the club. He was a partner in the Sam Nahm Co., a produce business. He was the oldest known graduate of the Bowling Green Business University. Mr. Cristal came to Bowling Green in 1882 from Memphis. In 1944 his diploma was still hanging in the Library of the Business University. He came to America from Odessa, Russia on the Black Sea. He married Miss Hettie Nahm, daughter of Sam Nahm, Sr., in 1892 and they had two sons. He was active in obtaining the Bowling Green Hospital and was on its first board of directors. He was a member of the Kentucky Society for Crippled Children and a Director of the Bowling Green Chamber of Commerce. Several years ago, the Bowling Green Rotary Club proclaimed Sam Cristal Day. At that meeting, a letter of commendation was given to him by each member. One member wrote "Mr. Cristal is regarded by his fellow Rotarians as probably being the best man in Bowling Green" At a study club meeting during World War I at which he was a guest the subject of Palestine came up. At the time there was a "Back to Jerusalem" movement. When Mr. Cristal was invited to participate in the discussion, he was asked: "Mr Cristal, do you want to return to Jerusalem? No he replied positively. I found my Jerusalem when I came to America as a poor boy and you took me in and gave me a chance to work and be happy. No, I don't want my bones to be taken to Jerusalem. I want to be buried in Fairview Cemetery." Members of the club rated that statement as one of the most patriotic of the war.

The club also received a certificate from the U.S. Treasury Department in 1944 commending the Club for its patriotic effort relating to the war bond drives. The certificate bore the signature of Henry Morganthau, Jr. There would be other war bond drives before the club reached its final total of eight.

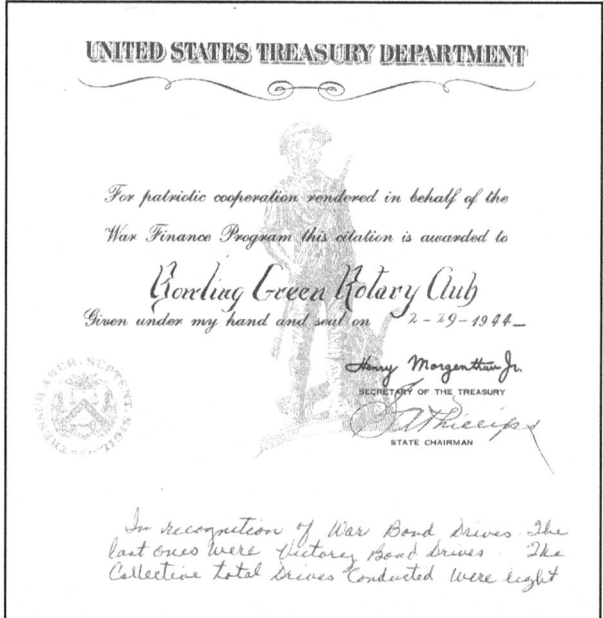

On November 7,1945, W.J. Craig (Uncle Billy) would be on the program. Early in 1946, Dr. J.T. Gilbert returned to the Club after several years of service to his country in the Medical Corp. Dr. Gilbert, remember, with his partner, Rotarian Dr. G. Y. Graves founded Graves-Gilbert Clinic. But let us not get ahead of ourselves. There was much for Rotary and the country and indeed the World to experience in 1945 before the aforementioned November events in Rotary.

On April 12,1945, while at Warm Springs, Georgia, President Roosevelt suffered a cerebral hemorrhage and died. For many, he was the only president they had ever known. He was a few months into his fourth term when his death occurred. This was an unprecedented tenure in the American presidency. The President had suffered polio in 1921 and had lost control of his lower limbs. With the help of leg braces, he battled back and was elected Governor of New York in 1928 and for a second term in 1930 by 725,000 votes. In 1932 he was elected to the first of his four terms as president. He was a very popular president. The events that he faced were mammoth – first to move in a direction to help the country recover from the depression that was in its midst. He and Congress instituted many social programs which became a safety net for the American people, including Social Security. Later in his tenure, he led the US and its Allies in prosecuting World War II to a successful conclusion. Every American, regardless of political party felt a great loss on April 12, 1945. The nation was grieved, but events were moving so rapidly that the country had a limited time to reflect. The War in Europe was moving rapidly toward a favorable conclusion for the U.S. and the Allied Forces. V.E. Day was celebrated on May 8, 1945. On August 6, 1945, a B29 called the "Enola Gay" dropped an atomic bomb on the city of Hiroshima and 3 days later another one on Nagasaki. The death and destruction was almost incomprehensible. The Japanese forces had no realistic choice but to surrender and on September 2, 1945 the Allies and Japan signed a surrender agreement aboard the US battleship *"The Missouri"* in Tokyo Bay. Three years, eight months and twenty-two days after Pearl Harbor, World War II ended.

On to 1946 again, P.C. Deemer, Jr. (flower retail) was introduced as a new

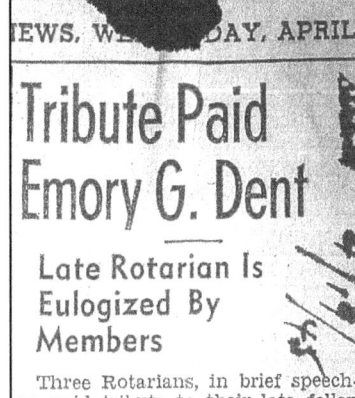

Tribute Paid Emory G. Dent

Late Rotarian Is Eulogized By Members

Three Rotarians, in brief speeches, paid tribute to their late fellow club member, Emory G. Dent, at the regular noon meeting of the club today, after which the organization adjourned following a moment of silent prayer.

J. L. Harman said that Mr. Dent was a man who "added sparkle to Rotary club meetings." He pointed out that he had assisted as many men and institutions as any man in the city.

L. B. Finn said that Mr. Dent typified the acme of Rotary ideals. W. S. Sumpter read a poem by the late Carl Herdman, which he said exactly summed up the life philosophy of Mr. Dent.

J. Murray Hill's motion that the addresses be recorded on Rotary stationery and sent to Mr Dent's widow, was adopted by the club.

Prior to the talks, the Rev. Fred P. Turner led in prayer for success of the San Francisco conference.

Guests were Capt. Mitchell Leichhardt, U. S. Army; Lieut. (jg) Chester Travelstead, U. S. Navy; Will Gooch Travelstead, Baltimore Petty Officer Alene Kasten, wave recruiter from the Cincinnati office; Chief S. C. Newman, local U. S. Navy recruiter and Rotarian N. C. "Pete" Hancock, of Russellville.

member, second to his father and John B. Gaines presented his brother, Ray Gaines, as a new member second to his father C.M. Gaines (Classification-Newspaper Publishing).

Back to August 29, 1944 Sam Cristal's (charter member) body was laid to rest in Fairview Cemetery (as he had so eloquently desired) in the city and the country that he so loved. In November of 1944, Dr. J. L. Harman chaired what must have been war bond drive #7. Rotary's quota was $132,000. The Club raised $177,000.

Emory Dent, a man with so much energy, and drive, died on April 19, 1945. He was the Dent of Carpenter-Dent-Sublett drug stores. He was born in Leitchfield, Ky. In 1904, Emory Dent married Miss Effie Carpenter, daughter of Tibbis Carpenter one of Mr. Dent's partners. In 1925, Harold W. Sublett became a member with Emory Dent and Tibbis Carpenter in the Bowling Green Stores – hence the CDS logo. The firm was founded in 1912. He was always interested in good roads and in that regard is probably known best for his identification with the Jackson Highway which runs between Chicago and New Orleans. It was built in 1915-1916. He was a member of the Kentucky State Highway Commission and served 2 years as State Highway Commissioner. He was very active in Rotary and chaired the Boys Work Committee and the Crippled Children Committee. Three Rotarians eulogized Dent: Rotarian Dr. J.L. Harman said that Mr. Dent added sparkle to Rotary, L. B. Finn said that Mr. Dent represented Rotary ideals and W.C. Sumpter read a poem by Carl Herdman in which he summed up the life philosophy of Mr. Dent. J. Murray Hill, Sr. moved that the address be recorded on Rotary stationary and sent to Mrs. Dent. The motion was adopted. On July 28, 1948, there was a joint meeting of Rotary, Kiwanis, and Lions. The joint meeting was preliminary to a visit to Bowling Green of the Freedom Train. The meeting was held at the Helm Hotel, and Ben Kilgore of Franklin was the speaker. The Freedom Train carried historical documents. Speaking at the official opening of Rededication week, Mr. Kilgore envisioned the train as more than a carrier of historical documents. It is a great revival, a revival to awaken our spirits and inspire us to be a greater nation. Mr. Kilgore was introduced by Bowling Green's J. David Francis. The train was to be displayed at the L & N depot at 401 Kentucky Street.

At the meeting on February 2,1949, volunteers to solicit for the bond issues for the hospital at Reservoir Park were solicited. The following members responded: Paul L. Garrett, Basil Pence, Paul Deemer, Jr., Alan Dodd, Dr. John McKissick, Lewie Harman, Jr., A.J. Miller and Maurice Hill. At the meeting of May 11, 1949, Joe McFarland Sr. was introduced as a new member. At the June 1,1949 meeting Dr. Paul Garrett requested a donation of $25 for Boys State, and, significantly, at this meeting, Dr. J. L. Harman announced that the dedication of the Emory G. Dent bridge across Barren River at State Street would be at 5:30 pm June 15,1949. Also, at the June 26,1949 meeting, President Wick Dotson made an announcement about establishing a fund for William (Bill) Osborne who lost both hands and his eyesight when a bomb (in a package) exploded at the local post office on February 2,1949 at 7:55 am.

[1]Architecture of Warren County Kentucky 1790-1940
[2]B.G. Scrapbook (Student Weekly) 2-6-1935
[16]The Medical Center at Bowling Green
[15]Kentucky State Highway Department District #3
[17]An Album of Early Bowling Green, Kentucky Landmarks by Irene Moss Sumpter

the 1950s

The Korean war came only five years after WWII to a war weary world in 1945 that thought it was through with war for a while. Korea was a single nation before World War II but the communists took over the North in 1945. The present two nations were formed in 1948. North Korea attacked the South on June 25, 1950. President Truman ordered air and naval forces to help defend South Korea on June 27th and ground troops were sent to South Korea on June 30th. The U. N. asked member nations to aid South Korea.

In 1950 letters went out to city and county high school principals informing them that the Rotarian Magazine and a report on the United Nations would be sent gratis to their schools. One of these principals was Mr. Carrol Brooks at Alvaton High School. Carroll Brooks later would become Dr. Carroll Brooks, M.D. and continued to be an integral part of this community. The committees of Rotary for 1951-1952 were Crippled Childrens, Attendance, Classification, Fellowship, Programs, Public Information, and Rotary Information. The President for that year was Dr. Ward Sumpter, Professor of Organic Chemistry at Western Kentucky State College. Ward was the son of longtime member W.C. (Uncle Billy) Sumpter. On July 11, 1951, the Rotary Club went on record recommending that the Western Trade School located in Bowling Green be continued for the benefit of the community. The trade or vocational school eventu-

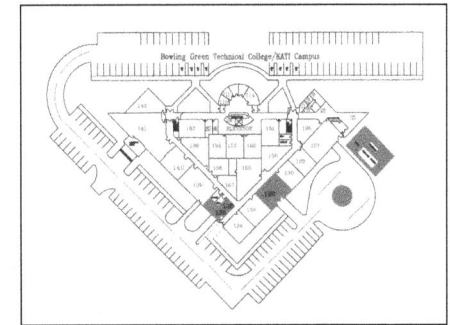

The 1950s

ally evolved into K.E.T.A.C., which it is today with a major education facility located on Morgantown Road in a beautiful futuristic headquarters building. It offers multiple academic and technical programs. Its last two presidents have been active members of Rotary. Dr. Jack Thomas headed up the school for many years and is still a member of Rotary, and Dr. Nathan Hodges, the present President, is an active Rotarian.

On April 10, 1952, the Club received a note from Coach E. A. Diddle. That read: Thanks for the messages you sent us during the NIT in New York City. The boys, Mr. Hornback and I really appreciated them. While we did not win, we really tried. As I always say "There will be another day". We are hoping, some day, to bring the trophy home. Signed Ed. Diddle.

In Korea, in the middle of 1950, the Allied troops under General Douglas McArthur were moving against the North very effectively, and had captured Pyongyang, the North's capital when on October 25th the Chinese crossed the Yalu and entered the war on behalf of the North. This changed the equation completely. In April of 1951 due to a disagreement on strategy, President Truman dismissed General McArthur and replaced him with General Matthew Ridgway. This caused quite a stir in the US. Truce talks began in July 1951. But as always seems to be the case, they were destined for starts and stops. Finally on July 27, 1953 a truce agreement was signed and the fighting ended. Korea is still divided into two countries in 2009, the dividing line being the 38th parallel.

In December 1953, at Christmas, the Club entertained its children with a Christmas party in the main dining room of the Helm. About 200 Rotarians and guests attended the luncheon, which featured a visit from Santa. In 1955, the Golden Anniversary of the founding of Rotary, our local club found ways to celebrate. Club President, Roland Fitch, Jr., wrote a letter to

Dr. J.L. Harman requesting that he write a history of the Bowling Green Club. President Fitch acknowledged that he was asking one of the busiest men in the club; but he also stated in the letter " You have been one of the most active members of the Club for many years- beginning 35 years ago". Dr. Harman responded to President Fitche's request by writing "A Brief Sketch of the Bowling Green Rotary Club". This small book was printed and is an important part of the Bowling Green Rotary Club archives. It has been invaluable to me in the preparation of this work.

The second thing that was significantly done to celebrate the 50th anniversary of Rotary was the celebration of the annual Ladies Night held at the Boots and Saddle club as a birthday dinner for the Rotary Club.

During the Korean war as indeed during World War II the activities of Rotary changed little despite the national concerns. Rotary continued its charities including a $175 yearly scholarship to Vanderbilt Hospital for three years to send a Warren County girl to study nursing. In that same year $1,000 was contributed to The Boys Club to buy a new station wagon. The Delafield Milk Program received $300 and the Little League $50. Other charities included funding a Boys State Delegate and

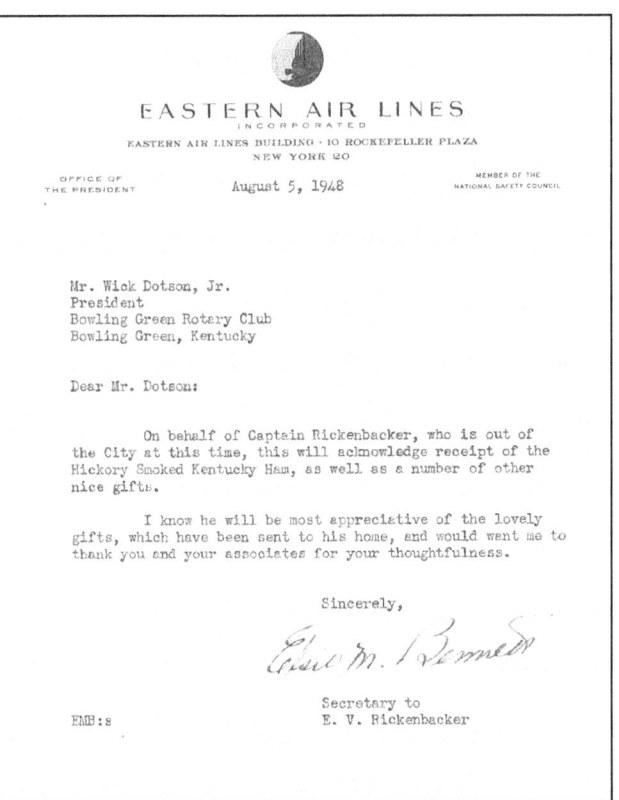

Irish girl was a youth exchange student at Western. Attention was continued for the improvement of 31-W, the Heart Fund and Crippled Children. An innovation that had become a part of the Bowling Green Club was the annual country Ham Show and sale which brings me to an interesting letter from the office of Eddie Rickenbacker. Captain Rickenbacker was the leading American Air ace in World War I having shot down 22 enemy planes and 4 balloons. He became President of Eastern Airlines in 1938 and was Chairman of the Board until 1963. The club had sent him a country ham in 1948. What prompted sending the ham? It could have been his association with Eastern Airlines which was the airline that served Bowling Green-Warren County for several years. There was later, a presentation of a country ham; this time in the 1960 Presidential campaign and that one was to John F. Kennedy when he visited Bowling Green during the campaign. The country ham came from the former Sam Nahm Co. operating as the Purina Feed Store and Country Ham Store. January 11,1956, E.O. "Buddy" Pearson addressed the Club on the proposed dam on the upper Barren River. Wililam Vogler read the resolution which asked the club to adopt the motion. The motion to adopt was read by Rotarian Herbert Jones Smith (immediate past president) and the motion carried. I assume this was the event that led up to the eventual building of Barren River Dam and Lake betweewn Glasgow and Scottsville.

On May 12, 1954, Dr. Stickles gave another one of his memorable programs – this time on the Indo-China situation. You will remember that this was the year of the defeat of the French at Dien Bien Phu. It also portended a relationship to the U.S. involvement in Vietnam.

March 14,1955 was a sad day for the Club. The death of past President Paul L. Garrett of WKSC and a past President of this Club had occurred on February 28,1955. The Club memorialized Dr. Garrett at the meeting and an eulogy statement by Dr. J. L. Harman, Sr. was adopted.

It was announced at the September 5,1956 meeting that next Monday evening the Inter-city meeting would be held at the Olde Fort Restaurant. One hundred twenty-one attended including those from the surrounding towns and in November 1956 club dues were raised to $7.

In February 1959, W.J. (Uncle Billy) Craig died. He was a charter member of this club, a past District Governor and the first secretary of the club.

April 4, 1959 Dr. Wade Weldon, 4th Street Methodist Church of Louisville urged his listeners to be for capitalism, not just against communism. And the thought for the week was "as old as man –the real destroyer of liberties of the people is he who spreads among them the bounties, donations and benefits."

On a happier note, the Club's own Herbert Jones Smith (future President of Rotary) was the recipient of the Junior Chamber of Commerce's Distinguished Service Award on January 27, 1954 ("Daily News" article). On this date, he was presented a bouquet of red roses by the Rotary Club in recognition of his achievement. The program included an explanation of the award by Jaycee President, Captain Fred Lane. Herbert Jones Smith was President of Rotary in 1955-1956 and served as acting Regent of Ogden College for many years.

Rotary Club Honors Herbert J. Smith

Herbert J. Smith, recipient of the Junior Chamber of Commerce's Distinguished Service Award, was honored at the luncheon meeting of the Rotary Club at the Helm Hotel today.

Smith, a Rotarian, was presented the award at a meeting of Jaycees last Friday. Today, he was presented a bouquet of red roses by the Rotary Club in recognition of his achievement.

The program included an explanation of the Distinguished Service Award given by Capt. Fred Lane, Jaycee president, and W. R. Draughon, chairman of the committee in charge of the project.

Introduced as a new member of the Rotary Club at today's meeting was Phares A. Hughes, head of the Metropolitan Life Insurance Company office here.

Guests at the luncheon were Mrs. Herbert Smith, Mrs. Roland Smith of Glasgow, mother of the award winner; Buil St. Clair, Falls of the Rough; Rotarian Ralph E. Knotts, Vincennes, Ind.; Tate Hutton, Chester M. Hock, Edgar Clark and Pal-

the 1960s

At the March 8, 1961 meeting, W.K. (Ken) Mullins was named President for the next Rotary year beginning July 1, 1961. Directors elected were Dr. L. O. Toomey, Dr. Luther Baxter and Guy Fuson. Charles Bryant was elected Vice-President. Garner B. Hanson, general manager of Mammoth Cave National Park, gave the program. Hanson told the Club that the old hotel building would be torn down within the next two years and that plans call for the addition of more lodge buildings and a camp store. The Bowling Green Rotary Club was instrumental in getting Mammoth Cave named a National Park, and Rotarian Dr. J.L. Harmon, Sr. even lobbied President Calvin Coolidge in this regard. The club was also involved in getting roads built connecting Mammoth Cave National Park to the outside world.

According to the "Park City Daily News" of August 10, 1961, Jerry Hornback age 25, and son of Rotary's own Ted Hornback was the recipient of a Foundation Scholarship to study in Dublin, Ireland. He left for Dublin

Mullins Named President Of Rotary Club

W. K. Mullins was named president of Bowling Green Rotary Club yesterday, and Charles Bryant was named vice-president.

At the noon meeting held at Olde Fort Restaurant, Garner B. Hanson, president and general manager of National Park Concessions, was the principal speaker.

S. C. Cooke was elected secretary of the club for the 37th consecutive term, and A. J. Miller was re-elected treasurer.

New directors include Mullins and Bryant, Dr. L. O. Toomey, Dr. Luther Baxter, and Guy Fuson.

Hanson told the club present plans call for the replacement within the next two years of the old Mammoth Cave Hotel, and that plans include the addition of more lodge buildings and a camp store.

Discussions are presently being carried on with architects preparatory to having plans drawn on the projects.

It is unlikely, according to Hanson, that there will ever be any facilities such as a swimming pool or golf course at the park since congressional policies emphasize conservation rather than recreation in the area.

Dr. William R. Hourigan, a member of the agriculture department at Western State College, was admitted to the club as a new member.

Guests included James Sherfey, Glasgow Rotarian, and Ed Pearsons, St. Louis.

The 1960s

THE PARK CITY DAILY NEWS, Bowling Green, Ky. 17
THURSDAY, AUGUST 10, 1961

(Daily News Photo)

KENTUCKY COLONEL Bert G. (Jerry) Hornback, second from left, displays commission presented him by Mayor R. D. Graham. The commission was presented at a Rotary Club luncheon yesterday at Olde Fort Restaurant. Hornback, winner of a Rotary Foundation Fellowship, was given a send-off by local Rotarians. He will leave Tuesday for University of Dublin. From left are Walter Nalback, Hornback, Graham, and Rotary president W. Mullins.

Under Rotary Fellowship

Hornback To Study At Dublin University

Bert G. (Jerry) Hornback, 25, yesterday was given a rousing sendoff by the Bowling Green Rotary Club as he prepared to leave for Ireland where he will study at University of Dublin on his recently — won Rotary Foundation Fellowship.

* * *

The Notre Dame graduate, son of Mr. and Mrs. Vernon T. (Ted) Hornback, 811 Covington Ave., was presented a Kentucky Colonel commission from the state government by Mayor R. D. Graham.

Rotarian Walter Nalbach praised Hornback as "the type of young man the club is proud to sponsor." The Bowling Green ary Club recommended Hornfor the fellowship — one of arded this year by the

foundation. He will leave for Dulin — via Montreal — next Tuday.

"You'll be hearing from m Hornback told the club membe "I'll keep in touch with the lo club."

Hornback graduated from We ern State College Training Sch in 1953. A Marine Corps veter he received his master's degr from Notre Dame this month. held a Navy ROTC scholarsh there during undergraduate yea and later received a gradua teaching fellowship.

* * *

Hornback will study literat at Dublin in preparation for a reer in university level edu tion.

Frank Melton, soil conser tionist assisted by Joe Por

...ildreth Wins Rotary Club Golf Tourney

Carroll Hildreth captured the annual Rotary Club golf tournament at Bowling Green Country Club yesterday with a gross 77, six strokes over par.

Low net awards went to J. H. Webb, Roland Fitch and B. C. Parker, all of whom had 71s.

Nineteen members of the club competed in the event.

Page 68 in Narrative

on Tuesday next. Jerry Hornback was a graduate of College Hi at Western. He was a Marine Corp Veteran. He held a Navy ROTC scholarship at Notre Dame during his undergraduate years and received his master's degree this month. Jerry Hornback studied literature in Dublin in preparation for a

Fort Restaurant Is Destroyed By Fire Today

Damage Set At $175,000

Olde Fort Restaurant was destroyed in a $175,000 fire early this morning despite efforts three companies of City Firemen to control the blaze.

* * *

Firemen were hampered in their work by the lack of fire hydrants close enough to the Louisville Road restaurant which would enable them to have a ready supply of water. The firefighters had only 300 gallons of water carried in the pumper unit. Work in fighting the fire was further hampered by a 26-degree temperature, extreme heat, and choking smoke.

The fire was discovered at 1:4 a. m. Two Central Station units, companies No. 1 and No. 2, answered the first alarm. After chopping through a door to gain entrance to the large stone building, firemen were confronted with stifling heat.

Making their way to the interior of the building, the firefighters went to the attic, finding it filled with smoke and flames. No sooner was one burning area extinguished than several others broke out.

Using Scott Air Packs (self contained breathing apparatus), the firemen fought the blaze in the attic until the supply of water in the pumpers were extinguished.

A second alarm was turned in at 2:18 a. m. and pumper company No. 4 from Cabell Drive Station was dispatched to the fire. By the time the unit arrived, the fire had broken through the roof of the building and within minutes, the entire interior was ablaze.

* * *

The restaurant is in a newly annexed area of the city that has no fire hydrants. After the water supply in the pumper tanks was exhausted, firemen could only stand by and keep watch on nearby buildings which were threatened.

One fireman said the building "might could have been saved."

FLAMES which early this morning gutted Olde Fort Restaurant break through the roof of the Louisville Road building. Within minutes after this picture was taken, the whole interior of the large building was an inferno which caused damage estimated at more than $175,000. For a period of more than an hour, the flames threatened nearby buildings, but the stone walls withstood the heat and contained the blaze.

(Daily News Photo)

Rotary Club To Meet 11/21/61 At Western Hills

Bowling Green Rotary Club will hold its regular weekly meeting at Western Hills Restaurant at noon tomorrow, Ken Mullins, president, announced today.

Change in the club's meeting place is the result of the destruction of Olde Fort restaurant by fire early today.

Business-University Ex-President Dies

James L. Harman, Sr., Was 86; Held Post At Bowling Green 25 Years Before Retiring

Special to The Courier-Journal

Bowling Green, Ky., July 11.—James Lewie Harman, Sr., 86, retired president of Bowling Green Business University, died Monday night at City-County Hospital.

He had been a patient there since suffering a heart attack June 13.

He resigned as chief administrator of the commercial school here in 1946. He maintained his association with the institution, however, serving as a member of the instructional staff until declining health forced him to curtail his activities this past year.

Was Honored In 1957

In 1957, he was elected the nation's outstanding commercial-school educator by the National Business Teachers Association.

Born in Allen County, Harman enrolled here at what was then Southern Normal School and Business University in 1893. He was graduated six years later.

He taught in country schools for a few years, then returned to Southern Normal and the Business University as a member of the faculty.

In 1907, the State took over the normal-school operation, and Harman and two associates —W. S. Ashby and J. S. Dickey —bought what became Bowling Green Business University.

Made President In 1921

Harman served as vice-president of the school until 1921, when he succeeded Dickey as president.

During his quarter century as president, Harman served for more than 10 years on the board of governors of the National Association of Accredited Commercial Schools.

He was one of five commissioners appointed by a Kentucky governor to survey the public-school system during this period, and was instrumental in selecting the sites for Murray and Morehead State colleges.

In recognition of his educational efforts, Harman was awarded an honorary doctor-of-laws degree by Kentucky Wesleyan College in 1932.

In addition to his life's work, Harman was a prominent lay member of The Methodist Church. For 50 years he was a member of the board of State Street Methodist Church, was a delegate to the annual Louisville conference 22 times, and was a delegate to the Methodist general conference four times.

He also had been a member of Bowling Green Rotary Club 40 years.

Wife Died In 1957

In 1900, he married the former Miss Nettie Kimberline of Washington County, who died in 1957. The couple had one son, James Lewie Harman, Jr., Bowling Green.

Also surviving are four sisters, Mrs. O. N. Wilson and the Misses Carrie, Jossie, and Bonie Harman, and a brother, Ray Harman, all of Bowling Green.

Funeral arrangements are incomplete.

University level career in education. After returning from Dublin he taught freshman English at Notre Dame while working on his doctorate.

In the early morning hours of November 21, 1961 the Olde Fort Restaurant was destroyed by fire. Firefighters were hampered by (the "Park City Daily News") lack of fire hydrants in the area, cold temperatures, and by the extreme heat of the fire. Olde Fort was the meeting place for the Bowling Green Rotary Club. On the day of the fire, it was announced that the Club would meet at Western Hills Restaurant at noon the following day.

Carrol Hildreth (joined Rotary 1957) won the annual Rotary Golf Tournament held on June 20, 1961 at Bowling Green Country Club with a gross of 77; six strokes over par. Low net awards went to Jake Barnard, Roland Fitch and B. C. Parker. Nineteen members of the club participated.

Two of Rotary's giants died — one in 1960 and one in 1961. Dr. J. L. Harman, Sr. died in July 1960 and J. Murray Hill, Sr. died January 27, 1961. Both men were former presidents of the Bowling

Green Business University.

Judge John B. Rodes gave the program on December 30, 1961. He was ninety-four years old. He paid tribute to Harold Sublett (85) and to A.M. Causey who also was ninety four. There have been a number of Father-Sons in Rotary. They were: Allen Dodd, Sr., Allen Dodd, Jr., J. Lewie Harman Sr. and Jr., J. Murray Hill, Sr. and Jr., W.C. Sumpter and his son, Ward Sumpter, Frank P. Moore, Sr. and Frank H. Moore, Jr., Paul C. Deemer, Sr and Jr., Roy Phillips and his son, Roy C. Phillips, Grover Holderfield and his son, Tommy Holderfield and C.H. Hildreth and his son Carrol and Carrol's son Mark Hildreth. And three of these Father-Son teams went on to become President of the Club. W. C. (Uncle Billy) Sumpter 1934-1935 and his son Ward was President in 1951-1952. Grover Holderfield was President in 1970-1971 and his son Tommy was President in 1987-1988. C.H. Hildreth was President in 1956-1957 and his son Carrol held the office in 1968-1969 and Carrol's son Mark and C.H. Hildreth's grandson was President in 2002-2003.

Some of the people who became members of Rotary in the 60's were: Dr.

John Scarborough who served as President in 1973-74. Others were Buddy Odom, Dr. Tom Baird, Bob Bueker, Henry Carlisle, Dr. Joe Cheek, David Cole, Dr. Keith Coverdale, Dr. Gene Farley, Dr. Lewis Graham, Charles Hardcastle, Bob Hovius, Tommy Hughes, Bill Hourigan, Bob Long, Ray Mullendore, William (Jerry) Parker, Henry Pepper, Dr. Nelson Rue, Ron Shrewsbury, Chuck Smith, Rev. Howard Surface, Lee Truman, Thomas Updike, Sr. and Dr. James O. Willoughby. Of these, besides John Scarborough, who became President of the Club were: Lewis Graham, Lee Truman, Jerry Parker, Henry Carlisle, Henry Pepper, David Cole, Charles Hardcastle and Ron Shrewsbury.

Six of the Club's members have become District Governor: They were William J. Craig, J. Murray Hill Sr., William Matthews, Dr. Walter Munday, Dr. Ward Sumpter, and William (Jerry) Parker.

J. Murray Hill, Sr. also attained the highest office of any Bowling Green Rotary Club member, when he served as R.I. Director and was twice sent by R.I. as a representative of Rotary to Europe and Asia.

No history would be complete without mentioning that in the ninety years that the Club has been in existence, at this writing, only four men have served as secretary: charter member, W. J. Craig, until 1925. Sam C. Cook from 1925 to 1971, Bob Long from 1971 until 2007 and presently Alan Vilines; truly a remarkable record. There have been four members who have had perfect attendance records for over 40 years: A.M. Causey 44 years and Lewis Graham and Tom Baird each had 46 years. When Kenneth Mullins died in 2006, he had 48 years. Other Clubs that the Bowling Green Club has helped charter are: Franklin, Scottsville, Russellville, Auburn, Horse Cave, Hodgenville, Glasgow and of course, the Bowling Green A.M. Club which will be discussed later.

In 1969, The Bowling Green Junior Womens Club initiated their Red Stocking Review and this review embraced a Maharaja contest. Historically, in India, the Maharaja was a Prince; therefore, the male selected as Maharaja was the Prince of the evening for the contest. In this contest, though, the Maharaja was determined by the candidate who raised the most money for the Junior Womens Club charities. Rotarians who won the honor were

Bob Eudy 1971, Grover Holderfield 1975, Tuffy Jeanette 1979, Tom Grogan 1980, Mike Buchanan 1981, Wally Moore 1982 and Craig Evans 1983. Others, who participated but did not win the title will be mentioned in the year in which they participated. It was a fun event for the community; was a good fundraiser for the Junior Womens Club and was a project of long duration. The Club's publication, has gone through numerous name changes. "The Pinion", "Rotoscript", The "Rotarian" and finally since about 1961 the "Cog". We talked early on about the Pinion and about what the word meant- a little wheel that interdigitates with a larger wheel as they turn. The "Cog" meant a tooth on the larger wheel that had many teeth or cogs. Usually the relationship between the local club and R.I. was the implication made by the names of the publication.

Inevitably, some professions produce more members than others; depending upon certain demographics. In Bowling Green, our club, probably has had the greatest number of classifications in two broad categories, namely in educators and in attorneys. These two groups have also made tremendous contributions to the Club. However, that was the purpose of classifications; to keep the club from becoming top heavy with any one business or profession. That insures diversity. So, the club has a broad general way of dealing with this eventuality that is fair to everyone. It is called the 10% rule. No group, as the two previously mentioned can comprise more than 10% of the total membership. I do not know of the Club ever having to invoke the rule, but it is there for us as need be. If it were to be invoked, the applicant would be told essentially that he or she would have to defer membership until that group fell below the magic number of 10%, at which point the Club would notify them.

Before World War II, Vietnam was a part of French Indochina, which also included Cambodia and Laos. During WWII, Japan occupied Indochina, but much of the area came under French control again after the war. Ho Chi Minh, Communist leader of the League for the Independence of Vietnam became head of the independent government in Northern Vietnam. Disagreement soon arose between France and Ho Chi Minh. Fighting broke out December 19, 1946 and continued for 8 years. The French were defeated in May 1954 at Dien Bien Phu and a peace agreement was arranged. A nine nation conference meeting in Geneva ended the war in Cambodia and Laos and divided Vietnam between North and South at the 17th parallel. The North was Communist and was ruled by Ho Chi Minh . It was called the Democratic Republic of Vietnam and the South became the Republic of Vietnam. Its president was Ngo Dinh Diem. The South had US backing. The US and the South did not sign the Geneva Accords but announced their intention to abide by them. The Viet Cong in the North was a guerilla group and had about 20,000 men. Some of them had been fighting about 20 years, first against the Japanese, then the French and finally against the Diem government.

The NLF (National Liberation Front) was organized in 1960. They were a political group organized to support the Viet Cong. The NLF set up councils in the South and built factories to manufacture weapons. Many of the VC's supplies came from the South. The VC became so strong that in 1961 the US had to choose between helping the South or letting it collapse. The US had 750 military advisers in Vietnam in 1961. President Kennedy ordered a step up in men and supplies. By February 1962 there were 2,700 US advisers. On July 30,1964 South Vietnamese naval craft raided islands north of the 17th parallel in the Gulf of Tonkin. Two US destroyers were patrolling nearby. North PT boats probably pursuing the South Vietnamese attacked the destroyers. Two PT boats were sunk. US planes then bombed the PT bases. This was the first attack on North Vietnamese territory. That prompted the US Gulf of Tonkin Resolution. President Johnson asked Congress for "power to take all necessary actions to repel any armed attack against US forces and prevent further aggression." The war had begun. There were 56,000 American deaths and in Aug. 1972 the last infantry man left Vietnam. There were 354 prisoners of war.

the 1970s

The 50th anniversary of the Rotary Club was held at the Paul L. Garrett Student Center at Western at 6:30 p.m. on September 19,1970. The Banquet celebrated the organization of the Club, September 1,1920. Two months after its organization, it was chartered. In honor of the founding more than 100 Rotarians and their wives attended; together with about seventy five Rotary dignitaries from the District. Speaker for the Banquet was Kenneth E. Wacker, a Director of Rotary International. Club President, Grover Holderfield, gave the welcome and Top Orendorf served as toastmaster. The invocation was given by Rotarian, Howard Surface, Rector of Christ Episcopal Church. There was recognition of Harold Sublett, a charter member, and Lon Causey as the Club's oldest member at age 100. Remarks were made by District Governor, Tom E. Bolton and presentation of entertainment was by past President, Carol Hildreth. Ward Sumpter, past District Governor, of Rotary District 671 introduced Mr. Wacker.

Ambassadorial Scholarships to study abroad for an academic year, are always at a premium — now being worth about $25,000. Equally as important as the monetary award is the life changing effect that it has on the individual. The ones of us who have served on the Scholarship Committee of District have had the chance to meet, look over the applications and hear the applicant's voice their hopes for the future. The applicants are an amazing group of young people. They are always gifted as to intellect and usually as to personality. They are true ambassadors to the world from the United States. The money, with which they are funded comes from the Rotary Foundation. Stephen Paige Smith, son of Mr. and Mrs E.M. Smith of Bowling Green, was chosen

The 1970s

by the District Ambassadorial Scholarship Committee in 1969 to represent Rotary and the local Club abroad (at Nottingham University in Nottingham, England for 1970-1971 school year). Steve was a history major with a minor in government at Western. Many factors went in to his selection. He had a 3.6 G.P.A. out of 4 and was involved in many extra-curricular activities including theater, a member of the Methodist Church and was a 1967 graduate of Bowling Green High School. Once Steve completed his year in England.

England Via Rotary

STEPHEN SMITH

A 20-year-old Western Kentucky University student will depart next Thursday for a 10-month stay in England and it all started with the Bowling Green Rotary Club last year.

It was in September, 1969, Stephen Smith, son of Mr. and Mrs. E. M. Smith, of 801 Wakefield Ave., was named a winner of a Rotary International scholarship for a year of undergraduate study at Nottingham University in Nottingham, England.

Smith was the only Bowling Green applicant to the local club, which forwarded his application to the District Rotary organization. From there, Smith's application traveled to Rotary International and he became a winner, one of 250 named by Rotary International.

While in England, Smith will make periodic reports to Rotary International, visit Rotary clubs in England and be an "occasional student" at Nottingham University.

At the school, students who attend but who won't graduate receive the occasional classification. When Smith returns next year to Western, he will begin work on his final year and plans call for graduation in May, 1972.

Smith will leave Louisville next Thursday for New York where he will board a TWA flight to London, England. According to young man, who majors in history and minors in government at Western, he doesn't care to think about a possible hijacking of his plane. The odds seem to be in his favor, he reasons, because of number of actual hijacks of all overseas flight, the fact a TWA plane already has been hijacked and simply because the flight is a New York to England flight.

Smith admits, however, he and probably many other passengers aboard the flight, will keep an eye for what might appear to be a would-be hijacker.

Once arriving in England, Smith will travel to Norwich, England, for a three-day orientation meeting of Rotary International scholarship winners.

Concluding the orientation on Sept. 27, Smith will go to Nottingham University, where he register for classes on Sept. 29. His plans call for taking the routine undergraduate courses at the school.

The Bowling Green man will remain in England for 10-months with spending his Christmas and Spring vacations travelling. The Rotary International will furnish him with a travel allowance.

Remaining until July, 1971, Smith, who is an only child, will be joined then by his parents, who will tour England and return with Smith to Bowling Green.

One of the main requirements of the scholarship is the winner isn't to marry during the scholarship period. If a winner should marry, he forfeits the scholarship and is required to reimburse Rotary International approximately $3,000.

But the Rotary International needn't expect a tidy $3,000 sum from Smith, who plans to complete his stay and return to Bowling Green single.

Many facets went into the selection of Smith for the honor and among them were his 3.6 scholastic standing at Western on a 4. system and his various extra-curricular activities.

He returned to Western for his senior year after which he planned to attend law school. Being one of 250 Rotary International Scholarship winners along with his high academic standing at Western did not hurt any.

On June 19, 1972, the Club voted $400 to send David Cole to the Rotary International Convention. Also, at an earlier Board meeting that year, the report was given that the Club had raised $1,360 in the fundraising campaign for needy children and on February 7, 1973, Tommy Hughes was named to represent the Club in the Maharaja contest of the Red Stocking review. Early Spring also produced the annual motion to nominate the entire club for Director.

Backtracking, the Board of Directors voted to host a recognition day for Sam Cook, longtime Secretary. Samuel Coombs (SC) Cook had only been a member of Rotary for one year when he became the Club's second secretary on July 1, 1925. He succeeded Charter member W.J. Craig. No one could have imagined at that time that Sam would serve, and with great distinction, for 46 years in this capacity. Sam retired June 30, 1971. Sam was born in 1895, served in the US Army during World War I, was active in the Presbyterian Church and was married to Elsie Burmeister Cook. They had two sons. Mrs. Cook was, for many years, Church Historian of the Presbyterian Church.

Sam Cook was a very efficient Secretary and the writer of this history is indebted to him and to his successor, Bob Long, for much of the archival material from which this history originated. Sam Cook died August 8, 1973 "(Daily News 1970)." On August 4, 1971 Jody Richards was voted into membership. On August 11, 1971 in a meeting at the Kentucky Belle, Charles M. Moore, Jr. became a member.

On November 24, 1971, a Food Committee was appointed to investigate changing the meeting place and on December 15, the Board voted that they would accept

The 1970s

the Committee's recommendation whatever it was. The Committee had been considering the Branding Iron Restaurant, which everyone knew had delicious food and would have been a popular choice, but it was not to be. Grover Holderfield, reporting for the Committee on January 26, 1972 reported. Past President Grover Holderfield reported that Mrs. Williams, owner of the Branding Iron, could not accommodate Rotary unless Kiwanis and Lions moved at the same time. Neither of these groups was willing to change meeting places at this time.

On February 16, 1972, Floyd Hays Ellis was chosen to represent Rotary in the Maharaja Contest that year.

Again the Club's meeting place was destroyed by fire. The Kentucky Belle Restaurant, designed as a replica of a Paddle Wheeler and very much like the Belle of Louisville was located behind the present day Mariah's (8th and State) on Eighth Street. The Club had met there for several years. This fire destroyed Rotary's flag collection, which was outstanding and had been started by Rotarian Dr. L. O. Toomey. (Dr. Toomey joined Rotary in 1953). The Kentucky Belle burned in June of 1973. The board met and unanimously decided to hold future meetings at the College Street Inn.

At the September 19, 1973 meeting, a donation of $1,000 to the Junior High's needy children was approved, and the Board decided that the Club would man the Salvation Army kettles on December 22, 1973.

In February 1974, Carroll Hildreth was selected to represent the Club in the Maharaja contest of the Red Stocking revue. And on March 6, Ward Sumpter nominated the entire Club for Director.

The annual Santa Claus for Children was set up for the third Wednesday in December. On March 26, 1975 officers elected were Harold Brantley, David Cole, Tom Hall, Tuffy Jeanette and Charles Owsley.

A.M. (Lon) Causey joined Rotary on April 28, 1928. He was a Butler County resident by birth and the son of Mr. and Mrs. Alfred Miller Causey. Lon attended Butler County Schools and later attended the Bowling Green Business University, then headed by H. H. Cherry, who later organized the Western Kentucky Normal School that is now Western Kentucky University. He was a veteran of the Spanish-American War of 1898. After his discharge he was employed by Western Union as a Morse Operator and manager of the Bowling Green Office where he continued for fifty-one years until his retirement. He and Mrs. Causey have one son, Dr. L. K. Causey of Bowling Green.

BG Rotary Club:
Banquet Launches 50th Year Observance

A Sept. 19 banquet, featuring a Bowling Green Rotary Club's Rotary International director as guest speaker, will kick off the observance of its 50th anniversary. Scheduled for 6:30 p.m. at the Paul L. Garrett Student Center at Western Kentucky University, the banquet will observe the founding of the local club in September, 1920. Two months after its organization, the club was chartered.

In honor of the founding of the club, more than 100 members and their wives will attend the banquet, which is by invitation only. Special invitations have been sent to approximately 75 persons, who include Rotary District dignataries.

Speaker for the banquet is Kenneth E. Wacker, of Winter Park, Fla. Wacker is a director of the Rotary International.

Also scheduled for the night's activities include entertainment by the "Club House Four," a barbershop quartet from Louisville. The quartet has won numerous national honors in quartet competitions.

During the program, Jo T. Orendorf will serve as master of ceremonies. Orendorf will speak briefly on the only living charter member of the club and on the oldest member.

The only surviving charter member is Harold Sublett while A. M. Causey, who will turn 100 this year, is the oldest club member.

Rotary president Grover Holderfield will welcome club members and guests to the banquet while Carrol Hildreth will introduce the entertainment.

The quartet will present comedy routines, which have been performed throughout the United States and Canada, during the Comminutes entertainment section of the banquet.

The "Club House Four" quartet was selected as cardinal district champions in 1962 and International Quartet finalist in 1963 and 1965.

Quartet members are Larry Knott, baritone, who is employed by Computer Aid; Joe Wise, lead, a music instructor in the Jefferson County school system; Shrader Miller, tenor, an attorney, and Tim Stivers, bass, a podiatrist.

Scheduled next on the program will be a talk by Wacker, the special speaker for the event. Wacker, named a director of Rotary Internationa for 1968-70, will speak on "Help Wanted—Leaders."

Dr. Ward Sumpter, one of five Bowling Green club members who is a past district governor, will introduce Wacker, the owner of a real estate and insurance agency in Winter Park, Fla.

Wacker also is a director of the Winter Park Federal Savings & Loan Association. An Indiana native, he attended Michigan State University and the University of Michigan.

A Rotarian since 1938, Wacker is a former member of the Rotary Club of Royal Oak, Mich., and presently is a member and past president of the Winter Park Rotary Club.

He has served as district governor, committee member and liaison of Rotary International. Besides being a director, he also is a member of the Rotary International districting committee for 1969-72 and liaison director of youth activities committee for 1969-70.

SPEAKER — Kenneth E. Wacker, a director of the Rotary International, will be guest speaker at the anniversary banquet of the Bowling Green Rotary Club Saturday. Wacker will speak on "Help Wanted—Leaders." The local club was organized in September, 1920.

He had a perfect attendance record for 44 years. Lon Causey was a regular letter to the Editor writer to the "Park City Daily News" and to the "Courier Journal". Rotary appropriately celebrated his 100th birthday.

The Children's Christmas Party was held on Dec. 17, 1975. The tradition continues and Ladies night was to be held at the Bowling Green Country Club on February 16, 1976.

On May 11, 1976, an agreement of intent was executed with the College Heights Foundation to give the foundation $500 each year for 10 years for scholarships for worthy students. Rotary's involvement with the Foundation was continuing to grow and would take several steps in that direction in the following years. Immediately, this would help fund Merit Scholarships for first year students at Western from our local city and county high schools. Rotary would give a $100 scholarship to one recipient from each of the 3 local high schools.

On August 17, 1976, the board voted to move the weekly meeting place to the Red Carpet Inn. The meal price was $3.50 per person. Dues were raised to fourteen dollars a month. The Children's Christmas Party was December 22, 1976. In the Christmas spirit, Rotary will, once again, participated in the Salvation Army Kettle Drive. At the December 16th, 1976 board meeting the board also agreed to print a history of the first 50 years of the Club at a cost of $2,500. This would be sold to the Club members for $12.50 each. On February 9, 1977 Ken Meredith, Sr. was named to participate in the Maharaja contest and on June 1, 1977 Tommy Holderfield was approved for membership.

On July 18, 1977, Rotarian and past District Governor, Ward Sumpter died and the Club, in grateful appreciation, agreed to hold a memorial service for him at the regular meeting on July 20, 1977.

In August 1977, it was announced that dues would be raised to $17.50 on September first. Back to the Club history, Nancy Baird, wife of Rotarian Dr. Tom Baird, was approached to do the history, but Judith Smith, wife of Steve Smith, ended up as the author.

On November 28, 1978, four new Rotary highway signs were erected.

The program on September 6, 1978 was furnished by WKU football coach Jimmy Feix, Bowling Green High School Coach Wilson Sears and our own Henry Pepper with his singing saw. Past President Grover Holderfield, who attended Pine Bluff, Arkansas High School and Arkansas A & M College, was named a director of Citizen's National Bank and on July 11, 1972, Lon Causey died at the age of 101. Lon's father voted twice for Abraham Lincoln. He had meant much to Rotary and the community over a long period of time.

the 1980s

For the Rotary year 1979-1980, Charles M. Moore, Jr. was president. Charles M. Moore, Jr. submitted his remembrances as President of Rotary, which follow:

Our Club was organized in 1920, so we were 60 years old the year I was President. Much more significant is the fact that Rotary International was founded in 1905 so, Rotary International was celebrating their 75th anniversary the year I was President of the local club. Much was done to recognize this significant milestone in Rotary history. We held a large dinner and dance at the Bowling Green Country Club and invited district governors, past district governors and all leadership of Rotary that was able to attend to be our guests at this particular event. It required quite a bit of planning and Mr. Top Orendorf served as Master of Ceremonies, and it was an event that was enjoyed by the entire community. In the archives of Rotary there is a video tape made of this particular event. This was new technology in 1979 and perhaps is the only Rotary event that has been recorded in full on tape. As indicated, this being the 75th anniversary of Rotary International, in the Spring of 1980, I was honored to attend the 75th anniversary celebration of Rotary International at the International Convention held that year in Chicago, Illinois because of course, this was where Rotary was founded. It was a great event and something that I will never forget attending. We were meeting at the Executive Inn and the above really are the highlights that I remember of my year as President.

The 1980s

In November of 1981, the club voted to support the candidacy of Dr. Lewis Graham for District Governor. The Club showed its great generosity by making many small contributions to charities late in the year. Some of these charitable contributions were to: The Girl's Club, The Boy's Club, Western Kentucky Gas Company, Letters from Children, St. Jude's Children's Hospital, Black and White television for Free Enterprise Fair, U.G.F. Small Fry Football, Welfare Board and purchased 144 cookbooks from the Cancer Society for resale to our members.

The entire membership was again nominated for Director for the next Rotary year and icon and community benefactor Ervin Houchens was granted waiver of attendance.

In the first quarter of 1982, the contributions continued to Warren 4-H, Child Protection, Bowling Green-Warren County Association of Mental Retardation, Little League Baseball, Boy Scouts of America, Big Brothers/Sisters and the Maharaja Contest as part of the Red Stocking Review.

Kenny Wallace was chosen to represent the Club at the R. I. Convention in Dallas on June 6-9. Officers elected for the 1982-1983 Rotary year were: Dr. Spero Kereiakes– President, Joe Cook– Vice-President, Frank Cole– Treasurer, Bob Long– Secretary. Elected to the Rotary Board were: Randy Capps, Joel Rogers, and Mike Hepp. Wally Moore was nominated to represent the Club in the Maharaja Contest in 1982.

In February of 1983, it was decided that the traditional raffle would be held and that the proceeds would be donated 60% to the Red Stocking Review and 40% to the Club treasury. Ladies night was to be at the Indian Hills Country Club on April 16,1983. In August dues were raised to $20 per month. Contributions to community groups continued in a generous manner. The Christmas Party for the Rotarian's children and grandchildren was scheduled for December 21,1983.

At the mid-December meeting, Joel Rogers was elected President, Mike Hepp Vice President, and Frank Cole and Bob Long were elected to treasurer and secretary respectively. The Rotary Scholarship funds with the College Heights Foundation continued to grow and then had a value of $6,752.17. In April 1984, the three past Presidents were appointed as a committee to nomi-

nate three members for Paul Harris Fellowships. One of these three to be elected by the Club membership.

Significantly on June 25, 1984, machinery was set in motion to establish a second Rotary Club in Bowling Green. Ken Meredith, Sr. seemed to have become resident expert in moving the Club through the process of chartering new clubs. The Club voted to limit the number that could transfer from our Club to the new Club, and on July 18, 1984, Ervin Houchens (joined Rotary 1937) contributed $500 in memory of Rotarian Clem Russell. The Club matched the gift and had Clem Russell named a Paul Harris Fellow.

On August 8, 1984, the Club voted to form the Bowling Green A.M. Club and to share the entire area with the A.M. Club as far as recruitment of members in the future.

The following Bowling Green Rotary Club members were to be transferred to the A.M. Club as of February 1, 1985. The charter had been issued –transferring members were: Mitchell Leichardt, George Patterson, Herbert Smith Sr., Roy

Rotary Clubs raise funds to wipe out polio worldwide

By JANICE BRATCHER
Daily News Special Writer

Rotary International, including the Bowling Green Noon and Breakfast Rotary clubs, has embarked on a new campaign, "Polioplus."

"We are out to eradicate six preventable communicable diseases that are still rampant in underdeveloped countries and we have decided to begin with polio," explained Bartley Hagerman, Rotary area coordinator for the project.

Hagerman said that although polio has been virtually eliminated in the United States, elsewhere the disease kills 75 children a day. By the end of the year, 27,500 children children will die and many more will be afflicted.

"The money for the project has come from donations and pledge cards filled out by Rotary members. We feel that Rotary International is uniquely qualified for this project because it has members all over the world. We have pledged to provide enough vaccine necessary for up to five years of consecutive immunization," Hagerman said.

Rotary will also make available to any country a team of experts to plan and implement the program. They will tap the resources of private business and professional sectors to do this, he said.

The current funding goal for the project nationwide is to raise $120 million. To date, the Bowling Green Noon Rotary Club has raised $23,000 and the Breakfast Rotary Club has raised $4,000. The clubs will accept contributions from the public; pledges may be be made by contacting any Rotary member.

"The "plus" in the Polioplus name stands for the other five diseases that we plan to wipe out after we finish with polio. These diseases are measles, whooping cough, diptheria, tuberculosis and tetanus," Hagerman added.

He stressed that all of the money raised from the Polioplus project will go toward the purchase of vaccine. None of the money will go for media and advertising campaigns.

The problem of communicable disease in the Third World is enormous. To imagine the number of children affected, Hagerman said to picture a 747 jetliner crash every hour of every day for an entire year. And the children die one by one from family to family.

"I can remember in the 1940s when there was such fear of polio in this country. No one would go swimming and they were afraid to shake hands for fear that they would catch the disease. I am very interested in seeing this kind of fear removed from the children in other countries."

Hammond, Jim Parrish, Sonny Barr, Harry Ford and Harvey Johnston. On January 19, 1987, Dr. Larry Pack was proposed by Dr. David Buchanan as a new member.

Again, significantly, Polio Plus made its advent, sponsored as a gargantuan project by Rotary International. You will recall that our Crippled Children's Program went back to about 1921-1922 and has been a consistent project of our Bowling Green Rotary Club. I am not sure what percentage of crippled children was due to polio, but it must have been very high. Before the polio vaccine became available, it was every parent's worst nightmare that their child or children would contract polio. The coming on line of a preventive vaccine was really the realization of the dream that we, as a club, had had perhaps unconsciously for many years.

Rotary International assigned monetary quotas to the different clubs around the world. Our Club assessment would be $12,000. The object of the Polio Plus was to eliminate Polio from the face of the earth by the year 2000. The local club chose Bart Hagerman to select a committee of 10 members to set a goal for the Club by November 1, 1987. On April 29, 1987, the Board set the goal for our Club at $50,000.

On May 4, 1987, the United States Supreme Court ruled that states with public accommodations laws on the books cannot discriminate on the basis of gender. Kentucky fell within that parameter and the stage was set for the admission of women as members of Rotary. In our own club this was not to be actualized until 1991 when we received our first application for membership by a woman.

The spate of Club contributions continued as follows: Special Olympics, Salvation Army and Warren Council for Literacy.

The College Heights Foundation advised Rotary that our original $500 contribution had been paid in full. However, if we continued our annual $500 contribution, the Foundation would match it with $300 and we will be able to give three ($330) scholarships to a recipient from each of the three city/county high schools. The corpus added about $100 to the totals. The Board voted to continue.

In June of 1985, the Bowling Green Rotary Club and the A.M. Rotary

Club voted to place new Rotary signs along the major thoroughfares leading into the city. This plan was presented by Mitchell Leichardt.

At the March 21,1988 board meeting, guests attending were past president Ken Mullins and Rotarian Joe McFarland. The guests were there to express concern about how the board members were elected. For many years they had been elected by someone nominating the entire membership as director. President Tommy Holderfield agreed to consult with other Clubs as to how they addressed this issue and get back to the board with acceptable alternatives. Numerous contributions continued and it was announced that we now had 19 Paul Harris Fellows in the Club.

The annual raffle continued and it was announced that this year's proceeds would go to "Arts in the Schools" program. The Club guarantees $1,000 and on October 17, 1988 the board discussed women in Rotary. So far, none had been proposed, but if and when a woman was proposed, she would be accorded the same consideration as a male applicant. And in November, Craig Evans discussed the program " Heal the Children". Judy Schwank and Nancy Lowery were in charge of the program "Heal the Children". The Club agreed to contribute $500 for Nancy to make the trip to Guatemala for this project.

Rotary again rang the bells for Salvation Army on December 17th and will contribute $500 to the Easter Seal Campaign for Crippled Children, and a lesser amount to Child Protection and the Warren County Council for Literacy. Again, significantly the Board voted to match up to $1,000 member contribution to the Bangladesh disaster fund.

Tommy Holderfield and the board apparently were not yet ready to change the way directors were elected (as recommended by Ken Mullins and Joe McFarland in March) because again the entire club was nominated for Director.

In July 1989, the board voted to make Walter B. Nalbach a Paul Harris Fellow and a consequent $1,000 contribution was made to the Foundation. Mr. Nalbach was a longstanding member of the Bowling Green Rotary Club and had rendered significant service over the years. In September of 1989, President Wade Markham expressed his desire to the board regarding the implementation of Adopt-A-Class. Later in September, the Country Club raised the meal price to $8.00. A committee was appointed to consider alternate meeting places. The Committee consisted of Bob Schulten, Ken Mullins, Larry Pack and Joe Taylor. In November, Jerry Parker nominated the entire membership for Director. The precedent continued with the election to be held on December 13 and the officers to be installed on the first Wednesday of July, 1990. On November 10, 1989, the appointed committee recommended staying at the country club. At the same meeting a contribution was made to the Girls Club and a $1,000 contribution was made to the Salvation Army.

the 1990s

On March 26,1990, Dan Cherry was voted a new member. Dan was a retired Brigadeer General in the United States Air Force and was destined to become a very active member in the community as well as in the Rotary Club. In Septembner 1990, it was announced that we now have 28 Paul Harris Fellows and on November 11,1990 a draft proposal of Adopt-A-Class was approved by the board and was presented to the membership for approval on January 9,1991. The original Adopt-A-Class committee was composed of Charles Hardcastle (the originator of the concept), Linda Thomas, Attorney and Col. Bob Spiller, United States Army, retired. The concept was to select a sixth grade class from an "at risk school", to assign Rotary mentors (one to each student) and to guarantee that their college education, at Western, would be paid for as long as they graduated from high school, kept out of trouble at school and with the law and maintained a GPA of 2.0. The club was assessed $5 per month, per member starting now to provide the money to finance the program.

The Persian Gulf War (2 August 1990-28 February 1991) was also known as the Gulf War, the first Gulf War or often as the second Gulf War and by Iraq's leader Saddam Hussein as the Mother of all Battles or commonly as Desert Storm. The final conflict was initiated with United Nations authorization by a coalition of 34 nations against Iraq with the expressed purpose of expelling Iraq from Kuwait after its invasion and annexation on August 2,1990. The U.S. furnished most of the forces, with Saudi Arabia, the United Kingdom and Egypt as other leading contributors in that order. When Iraq attacked Kuwait, it provoked the immediate preparation for war by the U.S., the United Kingdom, and Canada. The Conflict began on January 17,1991 with aerial bombardment and was followed by a ground assault on February 23 and was a decisive victory for the coalition forces. Operation Desert Storm was the US name for the air and land operations. Operation Desert Shield was the build up of coalition forces in Saudi Arabia in preparation for Desert Storm. Desert Shield was to protect Saudi Arabia. The US lost 294 (114 enemy fire). H. Norman Schaurzkopf was the US General in charge. The purpose of the war was to expel Iraqi forces from Kuwait. One hundred hours after the ground offensive began, President George H.W. Bush declared a cease fire and on April 6, 1991 declared that Kuwait had been liberated.

At the November meeting, a report to the Board was given by the Chair of the Scholarship Committee, Larry Pack. The administration of the scholarship program by the College Heights Foundation was discussed. The scholarships were given to one member of the graduation class of each of the high schools in the city and county – that number increased with the coming on line of Greenwood, bringing the total outlay of funds to $1,600 per year. That reflects an increase in the amount of each scholarship. On April 15, 1991, a contribution of $2,165 was made for children's car seats.

On June 17, 1991, new ground was broken when Linda Brown was approved as the first woman member of the Bowling Green Rotary Club and later that year the Club accepted its first non-Caucasian for membership. It had been an historic year.

January 8, 1992 saw the following elected for the 1992-1993 Rotary year; J. Craig Evans, president, Ron Schrewbury, Vice-President and Chuck Coates, Rick Dubose and Robert Soncrant Directors. The Club normally paid $600 for the president or president elect to attend the R.I. Convention. This year they agreed to pay in addition to the $600, the registration fee. In May of 1992, the Club had 17 members from Western and 20 attorneys.

On December 9, 1992, Rotarian Larry Pack read a resolution nominating Dr. Lewis Graham for District Governor of District 671 for Rotary year 1994-1995. The resolution was adopted unanimously. Rotary had $15,855.91 in its scholarship fund at the College Heights Foundation. The Annual Christmas party for the children was held on the last Wednesday before Christmas, and the Club was named 2nd place winner in the Salvation Army bell ringers.

On March 15, 1993, Ron Shrewsbury announced that Mr. and Mrs. W.A. Franklin, former principal of Bowling Green High School, had been involved in a very serious automobile accident. The board voted $500 to a fund for the Franklins.

In 1993, the Club was still contributing to camp Kysoc, a facility for crippled children sponsored by the Easter Seal Campaign. Backtracking a bit, two more women were approved for club membership. They were Vickie Elrod and Dr. Deborah Catron and on June 22, 1993 Edwin Gray Hurley became a member with classification Minister Protestant. He was Senior Pastor of the Presbyterian Church. In July of 1994, one of our women members went on the board. She was Debbie Catron. And in September of that year, the board unanimously endorsed the candidacy of William (Jerry) Parker, for District Governor of District 6710 for Rotary year 1996-1997. The resolution read "Be it resolved that William Jerry Parker, a member of this Club for 35 years, is in good standing and uniquely qualified for the high honor of serving Rotary District 6710 as Governor for the Rotary Year of 1996-1997".

Earlier in the year, Rotary had contributed $1,200 to Habitat for Humanity. Our own Regis O'Connor was in charge of Habitat and on November 11th of that year the Club contributed $2,000 to Child Protection.

On December 14, 1994 officers were elected for the 1995-1996 Rotary year. Chuck Coates was named president, Robert Soncrant was president-elect and Gary Dillard, Deborah Catron and Larry Pack were elected Directors. The Wednesday before Christmas, the Christmas party for the children was held as had become the tradition. Prior to that at the December 19th meeting $100 was contributed to Hospice in memory of Sonny Ennis and Joe Wilk. Remember Sonny's grandfather, Frank Ennis, was instrumental in the purchase, early on, of the Rotary Camp and chaired the Boys Work Committee.

On January 16, 1995, a committee was formed to study the feasibility of rewriting the by-laws of the Club. Appointed to the committee were: Gary Dillard, Chair, Chuck Coates, Larry Pack, Rick Dubose, Jerry Parker and

Bob Long. On February 20, 1995 Rex Galloway was named a Paul Harris Fellow by the Club and Dr. Hollis Gray was accorded the title, Honorary Member.

On March 22, 1995, on a motion by Larry Pack and a second by Bob Schulten, the new by-laws and constitution were adopted and on April 17 the board voted $975 to cover the air fare to Amsterdam, The Netherlands for our exchange student, Jeffery Keith.

On May 3, 1995, Dr. John Scarborough was reported to be very ill. David Hancock moved and Joe McFarland seconded that the Club make him an Honorary member. At the January 1996 meeting, Margaret Curtis was approved for membership and Dan Cherry was granted a leave of absence to serve as Justice Secretary for the State of Kentucky. In April, Patty Alford and Jane Manning were introduced as new members.

Jerry Parker was successful in his run for District Governor for District 6710 and served the district for the 1997-1998 Rotary year. The District Conference would be in Bowling Green in 1998.

In August 1996, inflation reared its ugly head again and member dues were raised to $45. The breakdown of the dues was meals $34.04, District and Rotary International Dues $5.00 and Adopt-A-Class $5.

The High School Scholarships were continued in the amount of $300 per awardee, one in each high school and in August of 1995, $2580 was contributed to the Easter Seal Campaign for Camp Kysoc and $1,060 was approved for Habitat.

In May of 1995, perfect attendance awards were named "The Dr. John Scarborough Award" upon motion by Debbie Catron and a second by Larry Pack.

On October 4, 1995, the committee to plan the 75th anniversary celebration was named. Larry Pack was named chair, together with members Jerry Parker, Bob Kleier, Ken Mullins, Vickie Elrod and Mark Hildreth. The Dinner was to be held November 1, 1995. Fifteen hundred dollars was appropriated for expenses. Each member was assessed $40.00 and this would be the only expense for the member and his or her guest. The Anniversary Dinner was held at the appointed date at the Bowling Green Country Club. The Bowl-

The 1990s

ing Green Rotary Club had been founded on September 1, 1920 and was chartered on November 1, 1920 by Rotary and the charter was presented to the Club on November 24, 1920. The 1995-1996 officers of the Bowling Green Rotary Club were Chuck Coates, President, Robert Soncrant Vice-President, Bob Long Secretary, Bob Schulten, Treasurer and Directors Rick Dubose, Gary Dillard, Deborah Catron and Larry Pack.

Dinner music was furnished by David and Martha Kelsey. The invocation was given by Rotarian Howard Surface, Rector of the Episcopal Church, who had also given the invocation at the 50th anniversary celebration. The welcome was given by President Elect, Robert Soncrant and the pledge by Director Gary Dillard. Soprano, Elizabeth Volkman sang the National Anthem accompanied by Martha Kelsey. The Master of Ceremonies for the event was Director Larry Pack. The presentation of Rotary dignitaries was done by our esteemed past President and District Governor elect, Jerry Parker. Elizabeth Volkman then sang "My Old Kentucky Home" accompanied by both David and Martha Kelsey. Jerry Parker then introduced the speakers. The first speaker was past President (1939-1940) Top Orendorf. Top had served as Master of Ceremonies at the 50th anniversary dinner in 1970. Top spoke on " The Bowling Green Rotary Club – Some of Its History". Jerry then introduced Tom Duncan Reed, past Rotary International Director and twice District Governor. The evening culminated with Elizabeth Volkman singing Vive le Rotary, and I am sure that the attendees joined in. It was a great evening, celebrating a great event in the life of our Rotary Club. The event was taped and is a part of the archival material of the Club.

In September of 1996, the Club suddenly found itself in red ink and the Board voted to borrow $10,000.00 to pay our R.I. and District dues and to stabilize the Clubs financial situation. On November 4, 1996, the treasurer reported a contribution of $9,305 had been made for Adopt-A- Class. We are now current. A discussion ensued regarding the internal accounting of the Club. Gary Dillard moved that an audit of the Club's accounts be conducted by three members of our Club who are CPA's. Bill Brantley seconded the motion, which was approved.

In December of 1996, Ben Smith was named to the board. He would later serve as President of the Club in 2000-2001. Since his tenure as President, Ben has become best known as Chair of the Children's Christmas Program each year.

January of 1997 began on a high note. It was approved by the board that the treasurer repay $5,000 of the $10,000 loan that the club had taken out, The Scholarship Fund with College Heights , at the end of the year 1996 amounted to $17,200 and that the Adopt-A-Class Fund had appreciated to $70,724.71. The board also established, in advance of selecting a new Treasurer, that his salary would be $250 a month. Larry Pack moved and Bill Brantley seconded that the Club name Rotarian Joe Taylor to the treasury post. The motion was agreed to. In July 1997, Gary Dillard assumed the Presidency of the Club. Gary summarized his presidency in 2009 for this publication. His summary is included below.

"During my term as President, we attempted to exemplify the meaning of Rotary as it was originated by Paul Harris. For one, we resumed reciting the Four Way Test following the meeting, which had not been done in several years. Second, we did our very best to see that we had interesting speakers.

The highlight of the term was having our own Jerry Parker serve as District Governor. We spent most of the second half of the year preparing for the District Conference. Governor Parker asked Chuck Coates and Larry Pack to chair the function. One week before the conference on April 18th, Bowling Green sustained a devastating hail storm. A number of visiting Rotarians continued to note the number of blue tarpaulins that kept most of our roofs from leaking.

Following much preparation and help from fellow Rotarians, we hosted a very successful conference. My personal highlight for the year was being named a Paul Harris Fellow by our club.

In December 1997, officers for Rotary year 1998-1999 were nominated. The president would be the first woman to serve as president of the Club, Deborah Catron, president elect would be Larry Pack, secretary, Bob Long and Treasurer, Joe W. Taylor, Sr. Directors would be Gary Dillard, Bill Brantley, Ben Smith and John Minton.

H.B. Clark of the Bowling Green Rotary Club was chosen to lead a Rotary International Group Study Exchange from District 6710 in Kentucky, USA to District 4470 in Brazil, during April and May of 1997. The team consisted of Clark, a telecommunications executive, Karol Kirby, an advertising director from Franklin Kentucky, Ann Cheuvront, an assistant Attorney General from Lexington, Terry Sebastain, a press secretary from Frankfort and Lori Farris, a consumer advocate from Frankfort.

The locations in Brazil 4470 were in the central highlands of Brazil and included the cities of Uberlandia, Araxa, Uberaba, Jatai, Goiania, and Caldas Novas and included a day trip to the capital city of Brasilia. The trip's main focus was a cultural exchange, with the team members living with host Rotarian families in each community, with days filled with exploring the local businesses and sights in this mostly agricultural area of Brazil.

There was also a vocational exchange component, and in most cities team members spent a day shadowing members of their own vocation in order to bring that experience back to the workplace.

The area visited was undeveloped from an infrastructure standpoint, with rough roads in the expansive area between communities, and being in the tropics, lack of any air-conditioning due to the incapacity of the power grid was noticed by all team members. Being away from the coastal communities, the English language was rarely heard, as the team members were immersed in Portuguese, the language of Brazil, with their host families.

The hosts went to great lengths to ensure that all American needs were taken care of and the team was well-fed! Friendships were made and the experiences in a foreign culture made lifelong impressions, both in the appreciation of the United States way of life and the understanding of an emerging market giant like Brazil. It was very refreshing to see that "Service Above Self" among Rotarians is universal and so obvious with community projects in the Brazil District 4470.

YEAR 145—NO. 176, 28 PAGES, 2 SECTIONS   Friday June 25, 1999   © 1999, News Publishing LLC

Serviceable advice

■ **BG attorney is named an adviser for national Rotary Foundation fund**

By DEBORAH RASCON
The Daily News

A solid, 39-year track record as a Rotary Club member has earned Bowling Green attorney Jerry Parker a new job with national prominence.

Parker, a member of Bowling Green Noon Rotary, has been named one of 28 national advisers for the Rotary Foundation's permanent fund and will represent Kentucky, Indiana and Ohio.

His experience as Rotary district governor, combined with nearly four decades as a volunteer fundraiser for the organization, helped land him the job, Rotary members John Osterlund and Dr. Deborah Catron said.

"He has distinguished himself and is a fine example of leadership," said Osterlund, the foundation's fund development manager. "He has proven himself to be dedicated to our objective and has done a fantastic job with promoting our endowment.

"Thanks to the fund-raising efforts of Jerry and his peers, we're approaching $200 million in our permanent fund."

Catron, president of Bowling Green Noon Rotary, wasn't surprised to learn of Parker's national appointment, she said.

"Jerry's an active participant in the Rotary and is very giving of his time," she said. "He's given much time to the local club and the district and now has been given a well-deserved opportunity to serve at the national level. He will represent the local area well."

Rotary International is a world-wide organization of business and professional leaders who provide humanitarian service, encourage high ethical standards and help build goodwill and peace. Founded in 1905 by Chicago lawyer Paul Harris, the club now boasts nearly 1.2 million members who meet weekly in 180 countries.

One of the organization's largest projects is stopping the spread of polio in economically developing nations. The group's PolioPlus program is trying to eradicate polio worldwide by 2005.

Since 1985, Rotary has raised $334 million to help protect more than one billion children from the

Attorney Jerry Parker displays the plaque he received when he was named a Paul Harris Fellow of Rotary International. Parker, a member of Bowling Green Noon Rotary, has received another Rotary honor – being named one of 28 national advisers for the Rotary Foundation's permanent fund.

> *I'm just a quarterback. It takes all of these other people to get involved and get the ball rolling.*
>
> — Jerry Parker
> Rotary Club member

virus, and millions of people in Africa, Asia and other Third World countries have been inoculated against polio because of Rotary efforts.

"When I was a kid growing up here in Bowling Green, polio was a scary thing," Parker said. "Once it started breaking out back in the '30s, they closed the swimming pools, and you couldn't get into the picture shows because of the fear of polio.

"We're trying to prevent a scare like that from ever happening again."

The Rotary Foundation is a not-for-profit corporation that supports Rotary International's efforts.

The foundation helps the club raise funds for PolioPlus and helps with other projects that improve the quality of life for people in developing countries by providing health care, clean water, food, education and other needs.

Other foundation projects include building 2,500 homes for people in Africa, providing funds for 1,200 students to study abroad each year and awarding grants to university teachers to teach in developing countries.

"Our motto of the permanent fund initiative is 'providing for tomorrow's need today,'" Parker said.

As a national adviser, Parker will visit other local clubs and help them identify potential major givers in their area. He also will advise the Rotary Foundation's trustees about which projects would be most successful and where.

"I'm just a quarterback," he said. "It takes all of these other people to get involved and get the ball rolling. It's a challenge because you've just got to be able to read the pulse of these people, but it's fun.

"What we're trying to do is promote local community service and international community service to make the world a little better and friendlier place to live in. I enthusiastically support this concept because it's one of the world's greatest philanthropic movements."

On December 15, 1997, the last meeting of the year, before the Christmas party, Alex Downing and Cheryl Allen were introduced. Alex was in later years to become President of the Club. Cheryl Allen was to become a very stalwart member and a leader in the community, as head of Community Action which inaugurated a public transportation system for the city.

At the February 14, 1998 board meeting the recommendations from the Adopt-A-Class advisory committee were read. They were:

A. Establish a permanent advisory committee
B. The scholarship would include a WKU Presidents Scholarship
C. The program would be expanded to vocational and technical training.
D. The Program would end for College in 2002 and for Vocational-Technical in 2001.

These recommendations were passed by the club membership on February 11, 1998. In May of 1998, the Club again contributed $250 to Camp Kysoc, the camp for crippled children through the Easter Seal Campaign.

In June of 1998, the board voted to donate $500 to Habitat in honor of Governor Jerry Parker and his wife Jane honoring his service to the local Club and as District Governor. And on September 1, 1998 the board voted to name a discovery committee to look into forming a foundation for the local Club. In August, $300 was voted for the Boy Scouts and in September

of 1998 the board voted memorial gifts for Roger Coates and for Kay Cole. It had been a very sad time for the Coates family and for the Cole family during the illnesses of these two. Roger was the college-age son of past President Chuck Coates and his wife Tina and Kay was the wife of past President David Cole. At the first meeting in July of 1999, Larry Pack became President of the Club and Mark Hildreth was named a new director, and on October 27,1999, Steve Wilson was named a new director to replace Bill Brantley who moved out of town. And on the eleventh of November, the Club adopted the millennium Adopt-A-Class. The Christmas party for the children and grandchildren of Rotarian's would again occur at the regular time in December. College Heights reported to the board that as of December 11,1999 the Rotary balance in Adopt-A-Class funds was $111,473.91. President Larry Pack appointed a Blue Ribbon Committee to make a recommendation regarding what to do with the residual Adopt-A-Class funds. The members of this committee were Jerry Parker, Chair, Charles Moore, Carroll Hildreth, Joe Taylor, Mike Manship, Rick Wilson and Bob Toth.

Let's backtrack to September 1999, when President Pack appointed a fundraising committee chaired by Jim Skaggs to raise funds necessary to build a Habitat House – the Club, besides providing funding would also furnish the labor. Other committee members were: Bob Spiller, Bill Brantley, Ben Smith, Jim Phillips, Phillip Clendenin and Charles Hardcastle. At the September 22nd meeting the president called on Jim to present the committee's plans to the club membership. Jim presented three alternatives to the Club that involved fundraisers. The plan was approved. Later about November, the subject had to be brought before the Club again due to the fact that Rotary, being a non-profit, had certain tax limitations that prevented us from proceeding in the agreed manner. It was discussed and agreed to that the project would be funded by each Rotarian that wanted to participate contributing $200 to the project. No one would be forced to contribute.

the 2000s

A Valentine's dinner and dance was announced for February 11, 2000 at the Country Club. This was something that had not been done for several years but had its origins in many Ladies nights, some of which were in conjunction with Valentines. Previously, Jerald Manning had been nominated for Director.

The Blue Ribbon Committee that the President, Larry Pack, appointed to decide what was best to do with the residual Adopt-A-Class fund made its report.

Recommendation #1 was that the funds would remain with the College Heights Foundation to be invested 60% equities and 40% bonds or fixed income. The residual funds as of July 1, 2000 amounted to approximately $120,000. It would be bifurcated at that time and funds for a second class would begin to accrue.

Recommendation #2 was that these funds from the first class would become a growth fund within the Foundation and would not be spent until the corpus had reached a level where the income would significantly fund scholarships to WKU or other universities. The Foundation would receive 1% for administration. The board adopted these recommendations. Early in his year as president, Larry Pack did an informal survey of the membership to determine how many members had played a musical instrument when students. A small group responded that they had and they began meeting to form a musical group to perform at Rotary functions. Richard Sowders, music director at the Episcopal Church, directed the group which besides Richard included Tommy Holderfield, Steve Wilson, Dave Gottfried and Rick Williams. The groups first Rotary performance was when they furnished the music for the Valentines dinner and dance in February 2000. They were an astounding success. Later, Richard relinquished the job as director and the group adopted the name of Skip Bond and the Fugitives (suggested by Tommy Holderfield). They changed to a format of light rock music and became a public entity. Even though they played at our annual Valentine's dinner and dances for about eight years, most of their performances were public events such as: Concerts in the Park Series in the summer, events at Lost River Cave and many varied events and entertainments in the community. As of this date, Skip Bond and the Fugitives are still going strong.

In the spring of 2000, Rotary thoughts, by necessity turned to Ambassadorial Scholarship candidates. It had been about 30 years since our Club had had a winner. Our candidate this year was a young lady from Western named LeAndra Celaya. She was a great candidate, with a high grade point average, was a Spirit Master at Western and had all the qualities that you would expect of an Ambassador. LeAndra won one of the scholarships in 2000 and the Bowling Green Rotary Club was back in the winner's circle after a long drought. This was only the beginning. In 2001, we fielded another young lady from Western. Her name was Brittany Long of Louisville. We were on a roll. The next year 2002, the Club's candidate was another Western student, but from Bowling Green. Her name was also Brittany Long, daughter of Mr. and Mrs. Curtis Long. Brittany Long was a great candidate but got squeezed out of the top three. She was a good trooper though and entered the race again the next year, in 2003. This time, Brittany Long won going away and did her academic year of study in Australia.

On May 31, 2000, President Larry gave a report to the membership regarding building a Habitat house. We had really done well with the fundraising but had come up a few thousand dollars short of the required amount. He reported that upon a motion by Ben Smith the board had voted to take the shortfall out of the general fund and go ahead and build the house. On a warm June day of 2000, a Saturday, an overwhelming number of the members met at the Habitat site with hammers and the raising of the walls and the hoisting of the rafters began. The structure of the house was completed

The 2000s

that day. It was a great day for Rotary, as well as, for Habitat. Nine years later, members still mention what a great experience that was for the Club.

The first Wednesday in July 2000, Ben Smith became president and one of the first things we did was to make a contribution to George Washington University in memory of Sterling Willoughby. One of the fondest memories of Sterling was that for years he was in charge of Rotary's ringing of the bells for the Salvation Army. Whatever the monetary worth to the Salvation Army, it restored the faith in the human family to participate in the event and to see the joy that it brought to the givers' faces when they contributed – especially the children.

Mac Jefferson (President in 2008-2009) took up the mantle for the proj-

---

History of the Salvation Army

William Booth embarked upon his ministerial career in 1852. His crusade was to win the lost multitudes of London to Christ. He went into the streets of London to preach the gospel of Jesus Christ to the poor, the homeless, the hungry and the destitute.

Booth abandoned the conventional concept of a church and a pulpit and took his message to the people. His fervor led to disagreement with the leaders of the church in London. They preferred traditional measures. As a result, he withdrew from the church and traveled throughout England conducting evangelistic meetings. His wife, Catherine, was a major force in the Salvation Army movement.

In 1865, William Booth was invited to hold a series of evangelistic meetings in the east of London. He set up a tent in a Quaker graveyard and his services became an instant success. This proved to be the end of his wanderings as an independent traveling evangelist. His renown as a religious leader spread throughout London. His followers were a vigorous group dedicated to fight for the souls of men and women.

Thieves, prostitutes, gamblers and drunkards were among Booth's first converts to Christianity. His congregations were desperately poor. He preached hope and salvation. His aim was to lead them to Christ and to link them to a church for further spiritual guidance. Even though they were converted, churches did not accept Booth's followers because of what they had been. Booth gave their lives direction in a spiritual manner and put them to work to save others who were like themselves. They too preached and sang in the streets as a living testimony to the power of God.

In 1867, Booth had only 10 full-time workers. By 1874, the numbers had grown to 1,000 volunteers and 42 evangelists. They served under the name "The Christian Mission." Booth assumed the title of a General Superintendent. His followers called him "General." Known as the "Hallelujah Army," the converts spread out of the east end of London into neighboring areas then to other cities.

Booth was reading a printer's proof of the 1878 Annual Report when he noticed the statement, "The Christian Mission under the Superintendancy's of the Rev. William Booth is a volunteer army." He crossed out the words "Volunteer Army" and penned in "Salvation Army." From those words came the basis of the foundation deed of The Salvation Army which was adopted in August of that same year.

Converts became soldiers in Christ and are known as Salvationists. They launched an offensive throughout the British Isles. In some instances there were real battles as organized gangs mocked and attacked soldiers as they went about their work. In spite of the violence and persecution, some 250,000 were converted under the ministry of the Salvationists between 1881 and 1885.

Meanwhile, the Army was gaining a foothold in the United States. Lieutenant Eliza Shirley had left England to join her parents who had migrated to America earlier in search of work. She held the first *meeting of The Salvation Army in America in Philadelphia in 1879. The Salvationists were received enthusiastically. Shirley wrote to General Booth begging for reinforcements. None were available at first. Glowing reports of the work in Philadelphia convinced Booth to send an official group to pioneer the work in America in 1880.*

On March 10, 1880, Commissioner George Scott Railton and seven women officers knelt on the dockside at Battery Park in New York City to give thanks for their safe arrival. This was to be their first official street meeting held in the United States. These pioneers were to be met with similar unfriendly actions, as was the case in Great Britain. They were ridiculed, arrested and attacked. Several officers and soldiers even gave their lives.

Three years later, Railton and the seven "Hallelujah Lassies" had expanded their operation into California, Connecticut, Indiana, Kentucky, Maryland, Massachusetts, Michigan, Missouri, New Jersey, New York, Ohio and Pennsylvania.

President Grover Cleveland received a delegation of Salvation Army officers in 1886 and gave the organization a warm personal endorsement. This was the first recognition from the White House that was to be followed by similar receptions from succeeding presidents of the United States.

Termed as the "invasion of the United States," The Salvation Army movement expanded rapidly to Canada, Australia, France, Switzerland, India, South Africa, Iceland and Germany. Currently in the United States there are more than 10,000 local neighborhood units, and the Salvation Army is active in virtually every corner of the world.

~Courtesy of Rotarian Salvation Army Major, Ed Binnix.

ect after Sterling's death. He has been on the Salvation Army Board for many years and has been a worthy successor to Sterling Willoughby.

The ringing of the bells at Christmas has been a tradition of the Bowling Green Rotary Club for many years, but is much more than a tradition. The local Salvation Army, as well as the extended organization, continues to feed the hungry, clothe the naked and generally provide sanctuary and hope to those in need.

Early in 2001 and continuing in Ben Smith's year in the sun, the John Scarborough Attendance Awards were presented. Ken Mullins in 2001 had 44 years of perfect attendance and the years were to continue to accrue for him. Dr. Tom Baird had 37 years of perfect attendance and would get to 46 years a week before his death in 2009. Dr. Louis Graham tied Tom that year with 37. Leroy Underwood, age 98, was in the Club until 2009. He moved from Bowling Green to Lexington that year to be closer to family, he had 25 years. Bob Kleier had 23. Each year, this was an impressive event that showed the commitment to Rotary by these members.

On March 23, 2001, it was decided that the Annual Raffle would be held April 11, 2001 to May 5, 2001. The proceeds would go to the Parker-Bennett School for playground equipment. For many years Tommy Holderfield and Steve Wilson conducted the Raffle. Later, Rick Williams and others assisted. It would be a good time to mention, in this regard that for many years, Patty Alford chaired the Valentine's Dinner Dance.

Dr. Ward Sumpter became the Club's first Paul Harris Fellow in 1976 and Dr. Tom Hall followed in 1980. This was something that was dear to the heart of Jerry Parker, who was honored by the foundation for his benevolence and untiring effort on behalf of the foundation. His heart's desire was to see every member of the Bowling Green Rotary Club become a Paul Harris Fellow. In December of 2000, Jerry prepared to match any contribution to RI for the next six months. On October 18, 2001 Jerry agreed to match any members $500 to become a Paul Harris Fellow with $500 by Jerry up to $25,000. The Club agreed to match Governor Parker's $500. This would raise $50,000 for the Foundation. Later, many of those that benefited from Jerry Parker's generosity pledged $500 to help someone else become a Paul

Harris fellow. Other members contributed varying amounts. For this project, Jim Skaggs contributed $2,000 in matching funds for the first of three contributions. Ken Mullins contributed another $1,000. $1,000 contributions were made in memory of Henry Baird and $1,000 for Charlotte Kleier. Margaret Curtis contributed $800 to help make two members Paul Harris fellows. Later John Grider committed to $500 per year for 5 years for matching funds and in 2008 committed another $500. Charles M. Moore, Jr. committed to $500, per year for matching funds indefinitely. In terms of levels of giving, Jim Skaggs has reached level six, John Grider, level 4, Joe Taylor, level 3, and Margaret Curtis, level 3. The Bowling Green Rotary Club now has 111 Paul Harris Fellows.

On September 11, 2001, 19 terrorists identified as belonging to the international terrorist group Al-Qaida, hijacked four commercial passenger jets that had departed from three U.S. airports: Boston, Newark, and Washington's Dulles. At 8:46 A.M. the first plane crashed into the North Tower of the World Trade Center in New York City. It was American Airlines Flight 11. At 9:03 A.M., United Flight 175 crashed into the South Tower. At 9:37 A.M. American Airlines Flight 77 crashed into the Pentagon. The fourth, United Flight 93, crashed in a field near Shanksville, Pennsylvania – the time was 10:03 am. The planes were headed for San Francisco and Los Angeles. The fourth plane's ultimate target was thought to be either the capital or the White House. Some of the passengers and crew attempted to take control of the fourth plane. The hijackers seeing they could not prevail, crashed the jet. Everyone on board all four planes was killed and many others who worked in the Twin Towers, as well as the Pentagon, perished. Both buildings of the Twin Towers collapsed within hours of the impact, and destroyed adjacent buildings. In total, 2,993 people, including the hijackers, were killed.

The U.S. responded by launching a "War on Terrorism," which included invading Afghanistan to depose the Taliban, who had harbored Al-Qaida. Another measure taken by the U.S. was enacting the "Patriot Act," which was passed by wide margins in both houses of Congress and by both parties and was signed into law by President George W. Bush. It increases the ability of law enforcement agencies to search telephone, e-mail, medical, financial

The 2000s

and other records and ceases restrictions on gathering foreign intelligence in the U.S. It also expands Treasury's Authority to regulate transactions involving foreign individuals and entities. It facilitates authorities in detaining and deporting immigrants suspected of terror-related acts and expands the definition of terrorism to include domestic terrorism. The bill had sunset provisions that would cause certain parts of it to expire in 2004. Other parts would expire at later dates. It has twice been revised.

On January 17, 2002 the death of longtime member Dr. James A. Willoughby was announced. A memorial gift of $100 was sent to the foundation. Also announced was that the Valentine's Dinner would be February 13, 2002 and that there would be a reception at the Bowling Green Country Club for all Paul Harris Fellows on February 15, 2002. The Millennium Adopt-A-Class was begun in the year 2000. This was our second class and more will be said about it later. At the end of 2000, the new fork of the bifurcated funds at the College Heights Foundation totaled $3,459.00. On June 21, 2001, Dr. Fogle Godby was named an honorary member.

July 12, 2001 was a sad day for Rotary. Rotarian Phillip Huddleston's death was announced. The Club mourned. The College Heights Foundation reported to the Club that as of September 31, 2001 the Club had what is now a bifurcated fund, $112,111.02 in the original Adopt-A-Class Fund and $12,596.06 in the Millennium Adopt-A-Class Fund, and $20,373.05 in the Scholarship Fund (for high school scholarship recipients).

At the meeting on March 28, 2002, new rules for classification were announced. The rules were simplified by having only two classifications – active or honorary. On June 27, 2002, Rotarian Jerry Parker expressed three concerns for the Club:

That every member become a Paul Harris Fellow.

That the Club plan a community project and complete it each year.

Discussed matching funds for the Bill Gates Contribution to eradicate polio.

In August, President Mark Hildreth presented the John Scarborough Awards for attendance. In October a nominating committee to nominate officers for Rotary year 2003-2004 was named. The committee was Steve Wilson, Larry Pack and Ben Smith. The Valentine's Party for 2003 was scheduled for February 15, and was chaired by Patty Alford and Jeanette Rayles.

Thad Jones, from the first Adopt-A-Class graduated from WKU at midterm commencement exercises. His mentor was Col. Bob Spiller. On November 27, 2002 Alex Downing was named a new director and on the third Wednesday in December the traditional Children's Christmas Party was held.

At the February Board meeting, Jim Skaggs again pledged matching funds for four new Paul Harris fellows. In April the Bowling Green Rotary Scholarship fund (provides a scholarship to one student from each of the city and county high schools each year) was combined with the Adopt-A-Class funds. The total value of the combined funds was $107,000. On December 31, 2003, this fund totaled 136,876.74. Earlier in 2003 there was a spate of contributions. $3,000 to Capitol Arts for Picnic Pops; $1,500 to send one of the upcoming presidents to RI Convention in Brisbane, Australia; and $500 to the Southern Kentucky Festival of Books.

Daily News

Western grad makes good on club's offer

Bowling Green Noon Rotary Club foots bill for local student's college education

By TAYLOR LOYAL
The Daily News
tloyal@bgdailynews.com/783-3243

It was an offer Thad Jones how they were doing in school, invite them to rotary club meetings and Christmas gatherings and organize fun events for the students.

"We believe it's an opportunity for young men and women to make a future for themselves," said retired Army Col. Robert Spiller, who mentored Jones. "I know that schools give encouragement, but for someone on the outside to give them encouragement ... that's what makes it spill over the top."

Spiller said he was quickly impressed by Jones' dedication to the program.

"He's got a drive," Spiller said. "When he begins a task, from my observation, he finishes it. He's got a spirit of excelling."

It was this spirit that separated Jones from many in his class. Over the years some of the students broke the agreement with the rotary club by getting suspended from school

or falling below the set grade-point average. Others weighed their options and decided the pact was no longer worth the hassle.

Of those four, only Jones remained. He majored in human resource management, maintained a high grade-point average and often worked two jobs – even though his tuition was being paid for.

Saturday, Jones received his diploma – but not without first saying "thank you" to the club that helped make it happen.

At a Dec. 11 rotary club luncheon, Jones spoke briefly. When he was finished, the crowd of rotarians erupted in applause.

"Everybody stood up and clapped long for him," Spiller said. "He's always been a sincere, dedicated young man. ... It's been a pleasure dealing with him over the years."

But the Bowling Green Noon Rotary Club may not be finished with Jones.

As he is kicking around the idea of getting a master's degree, the club is discussing the possibility of paying for it.

The 2000s

The first Wednesday in July saw the investiture of Rotarian Steve Wilson as President and it was announced that the Adopt-A-Class members (Millennium Adopt-A-Class) and the mentors would attend a football game at WKU on August 28. Also, the John Scarborough Awards for Attendance were announced and the Club was to have a Golf Tournament on September 17. It was later announced that the Golf Tournament produced income of $2,338.18 and that this amount would be contributed to Girls, Inc. The Board decided to award the winner of the speech contest $500, to hold the Christmas Party for the children on December 12, and have the annual Club Raffle in March of 2004 with proceeds going to the Girls Club.

Sadly, on November 26, 2003, longtime member Sterling Willoughby died. Remember, Sterling had become synonymous with the Salvation Army "ringing of the bells." Sterling was a gentle and good man. A memorial gift was sent to First Baptist Church in his memory. In August of 2004, the Board voted to participate in international service projects with five other clubs; Russellville, Elkton, Scottsville, Franklin, Auburn and the Bowling Green AM Club. The total amount raised was $6,249.50. The Scholarship Fund on December 31, 2004 was $140,710.31.

On June 23, 2005, Alex Downing reported to the Board $1,500. scholarships had been awarded to one recipient from each of the four high schools and on June 30, 2005 the Club contributed $12,000 to Polio Plus. These were matching funds for the Bill Gates Contribution.

The Bill and Melinda Gates Foundation had contributed 350 million dollars to Rotary for the final assault on polio if Rotary would match the gift with 200 million. Rotary asked individual Clubs to contribute $2,000 per year for three years.

On July 28, 2005, President Vickie Elrod and the Board voted to participate in an international project with Rotary International and District 6710. The project was to fund a hospital bed in Bangladesh. The total cost of the bed was $8,333. One-half would be paid by RI, one-fourth by district 6710, and one-fourth by the Bowling Green Club. Our one-fourth would amount to $2,085.

Effective September 1, 2005, Club member dues will be raised to $50.

This is a net increase of $5.00.

On January 14, 2006, longtime member Ken Mullins, past President, and John Scarborough Attendance awardee, died. Ken was a totally dedicated Rotarian. He will be missed.

The Valentine's Dinner-Dance would be February 9, 2006 at Bowling Green Country Club and the Annual Raffle would be in April.

In November of 2006, the Board voted to fund its second international project of the year. It was to fund six scholarships in six different villages in Kenya. The total cost would be $2,400. On December 14, 2006 the Board voted to participate in the Shoe Project for Nairobi, Kenya to the amount of $2,000. The Club sent a request to RI and District 6710 for matching funds.

On August 14, 2006, Rotary members chartered a bus and went to Frankfort to attend the investiture of Rotarian John D. Minton, Jr. as Justice of the Supreme Court of Kentucky. Two years later, in 2008, he was named Chief

Justice. It was a great day for those attending. Justice Minton seemed pleased that we attended and Speaker of the House, Rotarian Jody Richards, made sure that we saw all there was to see about the Capitol – especially the House Chamber. It not only was a great day for the attendees; it was a great day for Rotary and for the State of Kentucky.

Also, in December it was announced that the District Conference would be held in Bowling Green on May 18-19 of 2007. On June 13, 2007, Bob Long's retirement was announced effective June 30, 2007. Bob was only the third secretary that the club had ever had in nearly 90 years of existence. In fact, Bob and his predecessor, Sam Cook, had in total served 82 years as secretary – Sam 46 and Bob 36. W.J. Craig had served in this capacity the first four years. President Shannon Morgan performed admirably in organizing Bob's retirement event at the weekly meeting. The Club felt a great sense of gratitude to Bob and to his two predecessors. They have in many ways represented the strength of character and the durability of Rotary itself. It was one of those very special days at Rotary – one that we will all remember. The Club presented Bob with a laptop computer as a token of its appreciation. Rotarian Alan Vilines would replace Bob Long as secretary of the Club.

In May of 2007, Bowling Green High Schools' annual Rotary scholarship to Western Kentucky University was named the William J. Parker Memorial Scholarship.

In June of 2007, Charles Hardcastle, who was the originator of the Adopt-A-Class project, contributed a block of stock to Rotary for the Adopt-A-Class project on behalf of himself and his wife, Carolyn. It was understood that the College Heights Foundation would sell the stock and convert it to cash. Charles and Carolyn gave the contribution with three stipulations, which were:

1) That the Club sponsor a third Adopt-A-Class.
2) That the fund be designated the Charles and Carolyn Hardcastle Adopt-A-Class Scholarship Fund.
3) That the Club would be responsible for raising a matching $100,000 over the next five years.

When the stock was sold, it actually produced $100,114.00.

Twenty students of the Millennium Adopt-A-Class (the second class) qualified for admission to WKU. Ten would be admitted in the Fall. New President Mac Jefferson presided at the July 17, 2008 meeting. Rotarian Cheryl Kirby-Stokes came up with the idea of having a piggy bank for members to put money in each week. She implemented the project for a year and raised $3,000.

In June of 2008, Treasurer Joe Taylor announced his intention to step down from the job of treasurer at the end of the Rotary year. Joe had served with distinction for a number of years. The Club, as one, expressed its appreciation. Joe Taylor was replaced by Rotarian Kevin Counts, who served one year before Cliff Long replaced him as treasurer. At the end of 2008, the College Heights Foundation advised the Club that the endowed scholarship fund ended the year with $155,210.58.

Cheryl Kirby-Stokes was elected a new director to begin serving July 1, 2009. The Christmas program for the children would be December 17, 2009. Looking forward to 2009, it was announced that the Club's first Rotaract Club would be chartered at WKU in the spring of 2009. Rachel Phillips will coordinate the Club with our Club. Rachel later won one of the Ambassadorial Scholarships available through District 6710. She represented the Franklin, Kentucky Club. The Rotaract Club was formed under the tutelage of Rotarian Dr. Sally Ray and Rotarian Cheryl Kirby-Stokes and WKU education coordinator John Baker and WKU graduate assistant Rachel Phillips.

Roteract had sixteen charter members and the initial officers of the Club were Kayla Shelton, Sara Moore, Jade Lynn and Colton Wheery. The Chartering of this Rotaract Club occurred during the Presidency of Mac Jefferson. The stated objects of Rotaract are:

1) *To develop professional and leadership skills*
2) *To emphasize respect for the rights of others based on the worth of each individual*
3) *To recognize the dignity and value of all useful occupations as opportunities to serve.*
4) *To recognize, practice and promote ethical standards as leadership qualities and vocational responsibilities.*

5) To develop knowledge and understanding of the needs, problems and opportunities in the community and worldwide.

6) To provide opportunities for personal and group activities to serve the community and promote international understanding and goodwill toward all people.

Rotarian Rob Porter, led a GSE team to Brazil in the late spring of 2009. the following is Rob's account of that experience:

Our District 6710 sent a Group Study Exchange (GSE) to Brazil District 4480 during the period of May 10-June 6. Rob Porter, Bowling Green Rotary Club member was the team leader for this GSE trip. Porter is a Corporate Banker with JPMorganChase in Bowling Green. The purpose of the GSE is for sharing the cultural uniqueness of each country with each other. We found there were just as many ways the people of Brazil were like Americans, as there were differences.

Porter, along with the District GSE committee chose the 4 team members for this program from 13 applicants eligible for the trip (team members must be non-Rotarians, employed full-time in a career field, under 40 years old and healthy enough and willing to travel for a month). The team members were Kim Fleming on staff at Sullivan University in Louisville, Maria Purichia an English as a Second Language teacher in Mayfield, KY; Desiree Jones a business consultant for non-profit organizations in Louisville; and Megan Mortis of Henderson, who is the local marketing manager for Hospice.

The team visited the 4480 District which is an area in Sao Paulo State of Brazil just north of Sao Paulo in Southern Brazil. We flew into Sao Paulo (Sao Paulo has 16,000,000 residents and is one of the largest cities in the world). From there we then flew onto Rio Preto which is about the size and "feel" of Louisville, Ky. WE were met with a banner and an enthusiastic group welcoming us to Brazil. We then visited 6 other communities in the state of Sao Paulo including Ferdanopolis, Mount Apravisel, General Saldago, Santa Fe de Sul, Outaporango and Cataluva. Most of these communities were small towns similar to Bowl-

ing Green and Russellville located in mostly a farming area comprised of farms that produced latex rubber from trees, sugar cane for sugar and ethanol, coffee and cattle.

Rio Preto is also where the District Conference was held the weekend just after our arrival. The highlight of the District Conference was getting to meet the President of Rotary International who is from Korea. At the Conference, I was able to deliver our presentation in Portugese after much coaching from some Brazilians on our flight to Brazil, as well as, coaching from our GSE host Vladimir once we arrived. Taking the time to learn a language a little, really helped us connect with people in a more genuine way. However, we did have very good interpreters in each town to assist in the communication.

We were housed individually with Rotary families in each town which provided us with a very intimate view of Brazilian life. Most of the Rotarians of Brazil are in the upper class economically and socially and comprised of professionals, business owners and government employees. So most of our accommodations were very nice and we enjoyed the company of our host families as much as we did the visits to the "sights" of the community.

On a typical day, we would rise from bed about 6:30 am and prepare for the day beginning with breakfast with the host family. The breakfast was typically sliced fruit, sliced cheese and thinly sliced ham along with coffee and juice. The remaining part of the day would be visits to Hospitals, Schools, Universities, Government offices, farms (fazenda) and businesses interrupted for lunch generally with the Rotarians. The visits were an opportunity to share ideas and best practices and learn from one another about the economies and culture. The evening would be a visit to a Rotary Club where we would present our power point presentation about our group and the USA. Then there would be a dinner and drinks beginning about 9:00 pm for a couple hours.

The Brazilian Rotarians are generally the elite people of the communities including doctors, lawyers, government employees and officials and business owners. Typically, the clubs were smaller in number of members

(30-50) but very active. Many included both the husband and wife as members. Many had their own Rotary Club Building that was shared by all the different clubs in that town. They were very accommodating and engaging and very much wanted to show us how proud they were to have us here and to show us their community.

Brazil was very much like the USA in that people wanted their children to be well protected with healthcare, educated, get good jobs, own a home and have a family. Most Rotary families had cars and lived very similar lifestyles to US families. Their love of sports was evident and centered around the national sport, futebol (soccer). Most all kids at one time or another play the sport. The people are very fashion driven, especially the women, the shoes-particularly high heels, are worn all the time in business, social, family and casual settings. Due to the heat of the area (which is similar to South Florida) most people wore summer clothes year round.

The Brazilian Rotarians and most middle class and upper class families have either a nanny, housekeeper or both which adds to the affluent lifestyle of those who are so fortunate. The down side is that most of the domestic workers have little opportunity to move up in society due to the lack of equal access to education and training.

Some of the highlights were visiting sugar factories, non-government drug rehab "retreats", sugar cane factories, the farms we were on a farm more than one occasion, we were treated to horseback riding, the meeting of the Rotary International President at the District Conference and learning to communicate/speak the Portugese language.

Overall, this trip was the trip of a lifetime and I was so blessed to have the opportunity to not only see but "experience life" in a country much like ours but with enough differences to make it quite intriguing and enjoyable. And it made me realize the depth of the Rotary bond, it is so strong, so deep, so broad, as to transcend cultural and language obstacles. We were treated like rock stars with TV and radio interviews in many cities and were the subject of a newspaper article in each town we visited. In these interviews, Brazilians wanted to know what we thought of our *new President, Obama, and what we thought of their country.*

This experience allowed me to appreciate what an honor and responsibility being a Rotarian is. As a result, I am now more involved and enthusiastic about being a Rotarian rather than belonging to Rotary. I look forward to getting our club to be a host for the next GSE group opportunity as well as being a host family.

Epilogue

The story of the Bowling Green Rotary Club is a dynamic that continues to be lived out each Wednesday as we meet together. It is an ongoing story and a story that enriches the lives of our generation as it has other generations since its birth in 1920. As we enter the second decade of the twenty-first century, the life of our Rotary Club continues its vitality undiminished. The older members continue their attendance at the weekly meetings as they and all members redouble their efforts to repopulate the Club with new members who give every indication of possessing the qualities that will give continued strength to the Club and they, in turn, will be strengthened by the ideals and associations that they will be exposed to as a member. In ten years, 2020, this Club will celebrate its centennial. It will symbolize much. It will portend much more.

Profiles

Henry Hardin Cherry

Henry Hardin Cherry was born to George Washington Cherry and Frances Martha (Stahl) Cherry on November 16, 1864 on a Warren County farm. He received little formal education until 1886 when he began studies at the Southern Normal School in Bowling Green. He went to school only about 2 months per year. On January 22, 1885 he walked to Bowling Green with 8 inches of snow on the ground and entered Southern Normal School. His life was spent there from then on. He was soon on the faculty and in 1892, he and his brother, Thomas Crittenden Cherry purchased the failing school. Thanks to Cherry's promotional genius, the school grew from 28 students to nearly 700 in 1899 when he purchased Thomas's share of the school, and the institution became known as Southern Normal School and Business University. Cherry played a major part in 1906 in getting the Kentucky State Legislature to create two state normal schools – one in Bowling Green and one in Richmond. In June of 1906, he became the first president of Western Kentucky State Normal School. The school then moved to the top of the hill in 1911. The school granted its first Bachelor's Degree in 1924. The Normal designation was dropped in 1930. Dr. Cherry ran for governor in 1915 and 1919, but withdrew both times because expected support did not materialize. He married Miss Bessie Fayne in 1896 and they had three children. He died August 1, 1937 at the age of 72 and is buried in Bowling Green's Fairview Cemetery.

H.H. Cherry Bronze Statue Committee

Dr. M.C. Ford	L.T. Smith	Kelley Thompson
Dr. F.C. Grill	E.H. Canon	W.M. Pierce
W.J. Craig	Dr. A.M. Stickles	Miss Florence Scheider
Miss Margie Helm	Roy Seward	D. West Richards
W.L. Matthews, Sr.	George H. Moseley	Sterett Cuthbertson
Dr. J. L. Harman, Sr.		

The unveiling and dedication of the statue was November 16,1937. The laying of the cornerstone for Cherry Hall was Oct. 27th, 1936. The dedication of Cherry Hall was October 27, 1936. Classes began in the building, Sept. 1937.

W.J. Craig

W.J. Craig was born April 4, 1872 near Owensboro, KY. He married Miss Ethel Grant and they had one son. He was head of the Science Department of Western Kentucky State Normal School (later WKU). Professor Craig was a charter member of the Bowling Green Rotary Club having joined in 1920. He was the Club's first secretary serving from the Club's founding until 1925 when Sam Cooke took the helm as secretary. He was also the clubs first member to serve as District Governor. He had thirty five years of continuous membership. He was a professor at Western Kentucky State College for forty seven years.

Courtesy of *A Brief Sketch of the Bowling Green Rotary Club* by Dr. J. Lewis Harman, Jr. 1955.

A History of the Daily News

Founder, John B. Gaines.

Since joining the newspaper world in the 1800's, Bowling Green has been the birth site of approximately two dozen newspapers, some of which had short-term lives.

More than 130 years ago, 1854 to be exact, an ancestor of the "Daily News" was published for the first time. It began as a weekly and first was called the "Bowling Green Gazette" but later became the "Democrat". It was merged about the mid 1880's with the "Daily Times", which was founded in 1882 by the late John B. Gaines, grandfather of the present John B. and Ray Gaines.

With the merger, the main competitor of the "Daily Times" was the "Bowling Green Gazette", a morning paper. When the office of the Times, an afternoon paper, burned about 1885, Gaines purchased the "Gazette" and consolidated the two newspapers to establish a first class daily. He sold the "Daily Times" about 1899 to W. J. and J. G. Denhart. This publication continued until 1942.

In 1901 Gaines purchased a newspaper called "Weekly News" owned by E.C. Cooksey and made it a daily in 1902 under the name "Park City Daily News".

Born in 1908 was the "Bowling Green Messenger", which began as a weekly and became a daily. In 1917 Gaines purchased the "Messenger" and merged it with his newspaper. It is this paper which continues to be published by members of the Gaines family today as the "Daily News".

The "Daily News" was under the leadership of John B. Gaines until the mid 1920's. It then went into the hands of his son, Clarence, who was publisher until his death in 1947.

Clarence Gaines (CM) was a Rotarian and served as Vice President of the Club in 1934 – 1935. He was succeeded as publisher of the "Daily News" by his son, John B. Gaines who served in that capacity until his death in 2007 – a period of 60 years. John Gaines was a graduate of College High School and the University of Alabama. He joined Rotary in 1940. He and his wife, Mabel Sharp Davenport Gaines had three children: Pipes, Mollie and Mary.

In 1946, John introduced his brother Ray Gaines, Editor of the "Daily News" as a new member of Rotary, second to their father, Clarence M. Gaines. Ray was married to Elsie Harlow Gaines and they had two children, Janice and Joe. Ray was a graduate of College High School and the University of Alabama, as well. John B. Gaines' son, Pipes, joined the paper in 1966 and has been publisher for about 15 years. Pipes is a University of Kentucky graduate and a U.S. Army Veteran. He joined Rotary in 1977.

Pipes sons, Scott and Steve, are both employed at the paper as 5th generation Gaines family members. Scott is assistant publisher and Steve is Editorial Page Editor. Pipes sister, Mary Gaines Dunham retired from the paper two years ago.

Dr. James O. Carson

Dr. James O. Carson, EEN&T Specialist was a charter member of the Bowling Green Rotary Club and was the Club's second President. He later became an honorary member of the Club. He practiced his profession from early manhood until he was 89 years old dying suddenly at the end of a busy day as he was closing his office. He was a member of the American College of Surgeons, as well as, numerous professional organizations. He was listed in Who's Who in America. His office was located at 442 Main on the Main Street side of the square.

Courtesy of *A Brief Sketch of the Bowling Green Rotary Club,* printed in 1955 and authored by J. Lewie Harman, Sr.

Samuel Coombs (S.C.) Cook

Sam Cook joined Rotary in 1924 and became its second secretary in 1925 succeeding W.J. Craig. He served in that capacity for 46 years with distinction, retiring in 1971.

Born June 1, 1895 in Bowling Green, Cook served in the U.S. Army in World War I, including ten months in France. Sam Cook was an active member of the church, The Presbyterian Church, having served as an elder. He was married to the former Elsie Burmeister. Mrs. Cook was church historian of the Presbyterian Church for many years. They had two sons, Sam C. Cook, Jr. and Raymond B. Cook. The late Paul L. Garrett, past President of both Western and the Bowling Green Rotary Club characterized Cook as the family man of Rotary because of the amount of time Cook devoted to his sons. Sam Cook has been affirmed by all the past Presidents of this Rotary Club and District Governors of Rotary International in the most laudatory terms. Sam Cook died August 8, 1973.

Sam Cristal

Sam Cristal was a charter member of the Bowling Green Rotary Club. He was in the produce business with his father-in-law, Sam Nahm, Sr. He resided at 618 E. Main (The former Presbyterian manse). At one time he was the oldest known living graduate (1886) of the Bowling Green Business University and in 1944 his diploma still hung in the school library. Mr. Cristal came to America from Odessa, Russia. He and his wife, the former, Hettie Nahm, had two sons; Phillip Cristal and Charles Cristal. Sam Cristal was active in civic affairs and played an active part in the formation of the Bowling Green Hospital of which he served on the Board of Directors. He later was active in crippled children's work in Kentucky. He was honored by his fellow Rotarians by having 'Sam Cristal Day' proclaimed. One of his contemporary Rotarians declared Sam Cristal is probably the best man in Bowling Green. Sam Cristal died August 29, 1944 and is interred in Fairview Cemetery as was his wish.

Harold Watson Sublett

Harold Watson Sublett was born on a farm eight miles west of Bowling Green, March 26, 1880, on Morgantown Road. He was the son of Samuel Benson Sublett and Laura Dean Wiley Sublett. His birthday was March 26,1880. Harold Sublett moved to Bowling Green with his parents in 1888. He started working in a drug store owned by George Wilson. The store was located at Park Row and State Streets. That location was later occupied by F. W. Woolworth Company and in 2009 by a new BB&T bank. The CDS drug store chain was formed in 1912 with Tibbis Carpenter, Carpenter's son-in-law, Emory G. Dent and Harold Sublett. Mr. Sublett also served as Warren County Treasurer in 1915 and was on the City Council under Mayor John B. Rodes from 1929-1933. He was appointed Post-master in Bowling Green in 1940 and served nine years. He was married to Miss Bettie Buckner in 1907. They had two children.

Though not the oldest member of State Street Methodist church, he had been a member longer than anyone else at the time of Rotary's fiftieth anniversary in 1970.

Harold Sublett was one of the fifteen charter members of the Bowling Green Rotary Club. When he was ninety he still attended weekly Wednesday luncheons. He was recognized during the 50th anniversary dinner in 1970. He was the last surviving charter member. Harold Watson Sublett died September 1973.

George H. Moseley

George H. Moseley was born November 8, 1885 in Gallatin, Tennessee. He was married to Miss Martine Aull. They had two children, Mrs. Virginia Carveth and Mrs. George Anne Vogler (Mrs. William N. (Bill) Vogler). George joined Rotary in 1921. He owned the Troy Laundry located on the square on East Main and was a Bank Director. He was a past President of the Club serving 1937-1938. He brought great vitality to the Club and chaired numerous important committees. His residence was at River Terrace on Richardsville Rd. (KY 185).

Courtesy of *A Brief Sketch of the Bowling Green Rotary Club* by J. Lewis Harman, Sr. published in 1955.

James Lewie Harman, Sr.

J.L. Harman, Sr. was born June 18, 1874 at Meador, in Allen County. He was the son of Samuel Lewis Harman and Mary Hogan Harman. He attended Allen County schools and in 1898 was graduated from the Southern Normal School in Bowling Green. In 1900, he became an instructor at the Southern Normal School and Business University. Later, he became part owner of the private school. He was President of the Bowling Green Business University beginning in 1921 and served about a quarter century. He had previously served as Vice-President of the institution from 1907 until he became President. He was a Director of Potter-Matlock Bank and was awarded an honorary Doctor of Laws degree from Kentucky Wesleyan College in Winchester in 1932. Dr. Harman was a prominent lay member of the Methodist Church. For 50 years, he was a member of the Board of State Street Methodist Church. He was a member of the Bowling Green Rotary Club for 40 years. Western Kentucky State Normal School became a separate entity from the Business University in 1906 when Henry Hardin Cherry moved it to the hilltop and became its first President.

The Business University purchased by J. L. Harman, Sr., W.S. Ashby and J.S. Dickey, Jr. remained at its present location at 1149 College.

Dr. Harman had a farming operation and his favorite recreations were golf, traveling and hunting – especially bird hunting. He died at the age of 86 in 1960 and is interred in Fairview Cemetery.

Dr. T.O. Helm

Thomas Oliver Helm, Sr. was born May 5, 1859 at Little Muddy near Sugar Grove, in Butler County, Kentucky. He attended public schools in Butler County and at Auburn Kentucky Seminary. He received an A.B. Degree from Lincoln Institute in Illinois and his M.D. degree from the University of Louisville School of Medicine. He also studied medicine under the tutelage of Dr. D.P. Cartwright in Bowling Green, Kentucky. On December 4, 1888 he married Nellie Blakey. They were the parents of four children; John Blakey Helm, Thomas Oliver Helm, Jr., Harold Holmes Helm and Margie Helm. Blakey and Tom were professionals in Louisville, Kentucky, while Harold became president and chairman of the board of the Chemical Bank of New York City. Dr. T.O. Helm moved to Bowling Green in 1910 and purchased the Morehead House Hotel in 1915. The Oil boom of 1919 caused an influx of guests at the Morehead house. In 1923, Dr. Helm razed most of the Morehead House and replaced it with a modern hotel called aptly "The Helm Hotel". Both of these hotels occupied the north east corner of State Street and Main Avenue. Part of the Morehead house was retained as an annex to the Helm.

Dr. Helm practiced medicine in Auburn for 24 years. He was also prominent in road building especially, 31-W from Bowling Green to Park City. Dr. T. O. Helm was elected to membership in Rotary in 1923 with classification of Hotel Management.

The Helm Hotel opened with a dinner on Labor Day 1924. He was a member of Westminster Presbyterian Church (12th & State) where he was an elder. He was one of the organizers of the Bank of Auburn, Kentucky and served as its President for six years. He was also the President of Warren National Bank in Bowling Green Kentucky for two years until it merged with The American National Bank. All four of the Helm children were very successful in education and in business. The daughter, Margie Helm, who spent much of her long life in Bowling Green was a member of the first graduating class of Bowling Green High School in 1912. (There were 6 graduates in that first class). She was a graduate of Randolph-Macon in Lynchburg, Virginia and received a certificate from the Pratt Library School in 1922 and a masters degree in Library Science from the University of Chicago School of Library Science in 1933. She taught Latin and English at Bowling Green High School and was an assistant librarian at a branch of the New York City Library from 1919-1922. In 1922 she became assistant librarian at Western Kentucky State Teachers College and in 1923 head librarian. In 1956, she was named Director of Libraries at Western. In 1965, the main library moved to the new "Margie Helm Library". Miss Helm was the first woman to serve as elder at the Presbyterian Church in Bowling Green. Miss Margie Helm died December 19, 1991 at the age of 97. Her father, Dr. T.O. Helm, had died December 17, 1939.

Emory Dent

Emory Dent was born in Leitchfield, Kentucky (Grayson County) May 5th, 1878. He was the Dent of Carpenter-Dent-Sublett drugstore chain and was the son-in-law of Tibbis Carpenter who was the Carpenter of the same chain. He was associated with drug stores for over 40 years. He was associated with six drug stores in Bowling Green, as well as, two in other cities. His parents were Samuel R. Dent and Georgia Bassett Dent. Samuel R. Dent was a merchant in Leitchfield, Kentucky and a Democratic activist.

Following completion of public school in Leitchfield, Emory started working at a drugstore in Leitchfield, and on his nineteenth birthday bought an interest in the store. After three years he sold that interest and moved to Scottsville where he entered the drugstore business with the Carpenters. The business was then known as Carpenter-Dent Drug Co. Other stores were acquired in Bowling Green and one in Franklin, Kentucky. Some years later Mr. Carpenter and Mr. Dent were joined in business by Harold W. Sublett and became Carpenter-Dent and Sublett.

In 1904, Emory Dent married Miss Effie Carpenter, daughter of his partner, Tibbis Carpenter. Mr. Carpenter served in both the Kentucky State House of Representatives and the State Senate. He was a regent at the University of Kentucky. Emory Dent was a member of the Methodist Episcopal Church, the EQB Club (a Bowling Green Literary Club), the Pendennis Club of Louisville, as well as, the Bowling Green Rotary Club. He always maintained a close acquaintance with many Democratic political luminaries. He had maintained a strong interest in good roads since his identification with the building of the Jackson Highway from Chicago to New Orleans in 1915-1916. He was in Borneo in 1930 on one of his four trips around the world when word came that he had been appointed to the Kentucky State Highway Commission. He immediately cancelled the remainder of the trip and returned home. Before the building of the railroads in 1830-1840 two coach routes were built from Louisville to the Tennessee line. These roads ran from the old Galt House in Louisville to the Maxwell House in Nashville. One went via Bardstown, Glasgow and Scottsville to the Tennessee line (31-E); distance of 144 miles and had cost $970,000. The other, ran via the mouth of Salt River, Elizabethtown, Munfordville, Belle's Tavern, Bowling Green to Franklin (31W). In places the two roads were within four miles of each other. For some years the railroads took away with a considerable amount of the use of these roads. With the advent of mass produced cars, these roads became very important again.

The Kentucky General Assembly of 1920 designated about 4,000 miles of roads as state roads and created the present State Highway Commission turning these roads over to the Highway Commission to construct and maintain. Eleven hundred forty eight miles had been finished leaving less than 3,000 miles to be completed. A large part of this 3,000 had been graded and drained. All bridges and culverts have been built and only need to be surfaced. According to Emory Dent, who was on the front lines of the effort, a splendid foundation has been laid for a good system of state highways.

Locally, Mr. Dent was responsible for the 31-W Bypass and for the building of the bridge across Barren River that tied in with the North end of the Bypass and State Street and 31-W to the North. The bridge was completed in 1949 and was named the Emory G. Dent bridge. It replaced the Old College Street Bridge, which was built in 1926. There would not be another bridge across Barren River constructed until 1987, when the 68-80 bridge three blocks west of Emory G. Dent Bridge was completed. Mr. Dent had extensive real-estate holdings, including the Opera House at Main and College where CDS #1 occupied the ground floor. Emory Dent owned the exquisite Dent House on Nashville Rd., which was later occupied by the John Gaines family and still later by Chief Justice of the Kentucky Supreme Court, John D. Minton. as well as other properties in the business district. He was President of Barlow-Moore Tobacco Co. in Bowling Green, the Farmers Tobacco Warehouse Company a Director of Citizens National Bank and the Bowling Green Bank and Trust Company.

Emory Dent was a high energy person, whether chairing a committee of Rotary or serving on the State Highway Commission. He was a powerful advocate for progress and for all that is good and noble. He had an army of friends, many of whom were state and national public servants and many of whom were leaders of this community.

On April 20th, 1945 at the age of 67, Emory Dent died at his home on Nashville Rd. in Bowling Green. The funeral was at his beloved State Street Methodist Church. Interment was in Fairview Cemetery.

J. Murray Hill, Sr.

J. Murray Hill, Sr. was born in Rineyville, Hardin County, Kentucky on April 17, 1891. He attended elementary and secondary schools in Rineyville and at age twenty entered the Bowling Green Business University. After graduation, he taught accounting, law and salesmanship at the school. J. Murray Hill was Vice-President of B.U. for fourteen years. He was elevated to President of the Business University after the tenure of Dr. J. L. Harman, Sr. He married Miss Ruth Phillips in 1918, and they had four children. He joined Rotary in 1921 and his rise in Rotary International was meteoric. He was past President of the Bowling Green Rotary Club, a District Governor, a Director of Rotary International, and was twice sent by R.I. to represent it at Clubs in Europe, Africa and Asia. He addressed the Rotary clubs of Cairo, Jerusalem, London and several other English cities. He was a director of two Bowling Green Bank, had a farming operation and chaired numerous Rotary Committees. The family home at 1320 Park Street was originally the John H. Grider House. J. Murray Hill, Sr. died January 27, 1961, with interment in Fairview Cemetery.

From B.G. Scrapbook, Page 272 and the "Student Weekly" dated (February 6, 1935 and the "Daily News", January 27, 1961.)

Dr. A.M. Stickles

Arndt Mathis Stickles was born January 4, 1872 in Patricksburg, Indiana. He received his primary and secondary education in the Patricksburg School System. He received an AB Degree from Indiana University, as well as, an MA and a Ph.D. He also received a MA from Harvard where he held a teaching scholarship in 1909-1910. In 1908, he was invited to become head of the History Department at Western Kentucky State Normal School. He served in this capacity for 46 ½ years retiring in 1954 (which was a national record at that time, for longevity at an accredited institution of higher learning). He became a noted historian, teacher and author. His published works included "Elements of Government: Political Institutions, Local and National in the United States (1914)," "The Critical Court Struggle in Kentucky, 1819-1829," "Simon Bolivar Buckner: Borderland Knight" (1940), "The Story of Kentucky (co-authored with T.C. Cherry)," "Pioneer Kentucky from 1792-1800 Mirrored in the Kentucky Gazette" and "the Ruins of a Confederate Fort on the Campus of Western Kentucky State College."

Dr. Stickles married a native of Henderson, Kentucky, Miss Laura Gorden Chambers on July 26, 1911. They had three children: Elizabeth Hume Stickles, Harriet Henry Stickles and James Channing Stickles. Dr. Stickles was a member of the Presbyterian Church and the local Masonic Lodge, as well as, many professional organizations. He died on October 13, 1969 and is interred at Fairview Cemetery in Bowling Green beside his wife.

Max B. Nahm

Max Brunswick Nahm was born June 8, 1864 to Emmanuel and Rosa Brunswick Nahm. He was a graduate of Ogden College (AB 1883) and Princeton University (AB 1885). He married Miss Sunshine Friedman of Paducah Kentucky on January 21, 1892. They had one daughter, Emanie Nahm who married Walter E. Sachs of New York City. Emanie was a noted author. Emanie had one daughter, Jane Ellen Sachs Hode of Philadelphia. Mrs. Hode was the mother of the Nahms' three great grandchildren.

Max Nahm was a member of E. Nahm and Co., a mens clothing store located at 442 E. Main Street from 1887-1924. He was a founder and a Vice-President of Citizen's National Bank and a member of the Board of Directors for 57 years. He had been on the Board of Bowling Green Bank and Trust since 1911. He was a former director of the Federal Reserve Bank of Louisville and since 1924 had been a director of the Federal Reserve Bank of St. Louis. He was a charter member of the Mammoth Cave National Park Association, formed in 1924, and had served as its President.

As a member of the Federal Reserve, in the 1930's, he proclaimed that debt was the cause of depressions. He also said that there were two evils in the economy: 1. Good times and the absence of fear and 2. Bad times and the absence of hope. In a speech in Clarksville, Tennessee, C.W. Bailey, District Governor of Rotary, presented Max Nahm as a small town man with a world wide vision.

Max Brunswick Nahm died March 20, 1958 at the age of 93. His office was at 422 East Main and his home at 1403 College Street where he died. The wealthy financier was considered southern Kentucky's wealthiest citizen leaving an estate of $2,200,000; the bulk of which was left to his daughter Emanie Nahm Arling of New York City; with lesser amounts left to his granddaughter, Jane Ellen Sachs Hodes of Philadelphia and grants to his 3 great grandchildren for educational purposes. City-County Hospital received $20,000 and would have received the entire estate in the absence of heirs. Max Nahm impacted his home town, his state and the nation in ways that few can match. Max Nahm was interred in Fairview Cemetery beside his wife, Sunshine, who died in 1937.

The Bowling Green Business University

The Business School was established in 1874. In 1884, Southern Normal School, which was located in Glasgow, Kentucky bought the Business University property located at 1149 College Street in Bowling Green and moved the Southern Normal School to that location. In the following years, there were really two schools functioning under one roof. The school became known as the Southern Normal School and Business University. In 1907, H.H. Cherry moved the Normal School operation to the hilltop, where Cherry Hall now stands and sold the Business University to J.L. Harman, Sr., J.S. Dickey and W.S. Ashby. J.S. Dickey became President of the Business University and served in that capacity until his death in 1921, at which time J. L. Harmon, Sr. became President. Dr. Harman had been Vice-President during J.S. Dickey's presidency. Dr. Harmon's presidency lasted about twenty-five years. He stepped down in 1945. At this time, the school was placed in the hands of a non-profit organization and its name was changed to the Bowling Green College of Commerce. The enrollment at the time of the incorporation was 800 students. The school merged with Western Kentucky University in 1963.

Ogden College

Ogden College, founded in 1877, became part of Western in 1928. It was endowed by Robert W. Ogden, a Warren County businessman, who died in 1873. He bequeathed $50,000 for a local college and a similar sum for scholarships for Warren County and Kentucky boys called the Ogden Fund. The Methodist Episcopal Church had operated a prep school on the grounds from 1872 to 1876. Hector Loving served as regent of Ogden College and trustee until his death in 1913. Two buildings and 7 or 8 acres of land overlooking Bowling Green were rented in 1877 and then purchased from the church by Ogden College. The church operated Warren College, a prep school on the grounds but closed it when plans were announced to offer tuition free education at Ogden. Prep & College curriculum were offered but 80% of the first class was beneath college level. Ogden's property was leased to Western in 1927 at no cost for 20 years. A scholarship fund was established for Western students and Western named the area Ogden Department of Science. The lease was extended in 1947 and 1956. On June 1, 1960 a 99 year lease was executed.

Potter College

The Bowling Green Female Academy was chartered in 1834. It met in the basement of the newly built Presbyterian Church located at 10th Avenue and State Streets. It was started by Franklin Jones and his wife, Mary Kendall Jones from Massachusetts. Soon, Mary Kendall Jones closed the Female Academy and established another school in a large Georgian Style mansion southwest of the public square. This was the Bowling Green Female College which operated for about 20 years. It closed in 1884 with the advent of a public school system. Next came the Southern Normal School and Business College, which moved to Bowling Green from Glasgow. Pleasant J. Potter College (Potter College) was located atop Vinegar Hill (now College Hill) roughly where Cherry Hall now stands. It was the Potter College of Liberal Arts. When Potter College first opened on September 9, 1889, it occupied the Potter Opera House on Summer (now College Street). As soon as the building was completed, the school moved to the hilltop location. Benjamin Cabell was head of Potter College. The first commencement was in 1890. Potter College of the Humanities (now Potter College of the Arts and Letters) became part of Western Kentucky State Normal School in 1928. Soon 15th Street was opened in front of the college. It was first called College Street, but was soon called 15th Street and Summer Street which ran from the Public Square to the top of the hill, one half mile, then became College Street. This all occurred in 1890. By 1891, Cabell had built a fence around Potter College. The greater accessibility of town, the proximity of Ogden College and the still prevalent wilderness of Vinegar Hill dictated additional refinements. The fence was a meaningful dividing line between: commerce and culture, risk and safety, nature and civilization and male and female.

Potter College was incorporated in Warren County and had a Board of Trustees. Both Potter College and Ogden College became a part of Western Kentucky State Normal School in 1928.

Courtesy of *The Mighty Band of Maidens* by Lynn E. Niedermeier

Dr. Ward Cullen Sumpter

Ward Sumpter was first mentioned in the Club's archival records as a guest of the Club on December 23, 1925. He was a guest of his father, W.C., "Uncle Billy," Sumpter (joined Rotary in October 1921). Ward was to become a member of Rotary in 1947 at the age of 44. Ward was a professor of Organic Chemistry at W.K.U. He served as President of the Rotary Club in 1951-1952 following his father's footsteps (who had served as President in 1934-1935). Ward also served as District Governor (one of 6 to so serve, as of this writing in 2009). He became the club's first Paul Harris Fellow in 1976. In 1977 the club named one of its Rotary Scholarships "The Past District Governor Ward C. Sumpter Rotary Scholarship". In the resolution naming the scholarship in his honor, it speaks to the fellowship, enthusiasm and nudging support Ward Sumpter brought to the club over a period of many years. Ward Sumpter died July 18, 1977.

Robert C. (Bob) Long

Bob Long joined the Rotary in 1960. He wass married to the former Jane Phalan and they have three children; Cliff Long, Brenda Long and Patricia Long. Bob has served on the Attendance Committee, the Classification Committee and as a Salvation Army Bell ringer. On the district level, he has served on a committee to elect a District Governor during Jerry Parker's tenure as District Governor. By far, his greatest service to Rotary has been as Secretary of the Bowling Green Rotary Club from 1971-2007. Bob has received Rotary Internationals "Commitment to Service" Award. This award was instituted by Rotary International's President Estes to help celebrate Rotary International Centennial in 2005. Only five Rotarians in District 6710 have received this award. After Bob's retirement as secretary of the Bowling Green Rotary on June 30, 2007 after 36 years of service, it was Bob Long's Day celebrated at the regular weekly meeting. Besides the accolades Bob was presented a laptop computer as a token of the Clubs appreciation for his service and as a testimonial of the Club's esteem for him as a fellow Rotarian.

Charles A. Hardcastle

Charlie Hardcastle was born at Alvaton, Warren County, Kentucky on November 11, 1932. He was educated in the Warren County School System and received his B.A. Degree from Western Kentucky University. He is married to Carolyn Kolar Hardcastle and they have two daughters. He served in the U.S. Army from 1955-1957 rising to the rank of Captain. His reserve unit was recalled in 1961 and he served with it from 1961 to 1962. Charles A. Hardcastle served as Mayor of Bowling Green 1984-1988. He joined Rotary in 1969 and served as president in 1980-1981. He furnished the inspiration for Adopt-A-Class and he and his wife, Carolyn, made a major financial contribution to Adopt-A-Class in 2007 in the name of Charles and Carolyn Hardcastle Adopt-A-Class Scholarship Fund. Charles is a Paul Harris Fellow.

He is President of Bowling Green Chemicals and Consolidated Paper Group and has been named a member of the Junior Achievement Hall of Fame. Charlie has served on the Board of Directors of numerous corporations, including Delta Dental of Kentucky. He is a past-president of the War Memorial Boys Club and the BG-Warren County Community Education Board.

William J. (Jerry) Parker

William Jerry Parker was born in Bowling Green on September 11, 1932. He was the son of Joseph B. and Ruby S. Parker. Mrs. Ruby S. Parker was a public school teacher and principal for many years. She instilled in Jerry the need for public service at an early age. Jerry held a B.A. degree from Western Kentucky State College and a J.D. Degree from Vanderbilt University. He practiced law in Bowling Green for about 50 years. In 1980, he was president of the Kentucky Bar Association. He served in the United States Air Force as a B-52 crew member and was discharged with the rank of Captain. Jerry joined the Bowling Green Rotary Club in 1960 and served as President of the Club 1969-1970. Jerry served as District Governor in 1996-1997 with great distinction. He was a strong supporter of the Foundation and contributed to it strongly in monetary ways during the ensuing years after his year as District Governor Jerry contributed up to $25,000 in matching funds to make as many as possible of our Club members, Paul Harris Fellows. His wish was for every member to become a Paul Harris Fellow. Jerry served on many boards and philanthropic organizations in the community and has served since 1978 on the Board of the College Heights Foundation at Western Kentucky University. In Rotary he represented Service Above Self in so many ways and exemplified the Four Way Test. Jerry was a Rotarian's Rotarian.

Jerry was married to the former Jane Martin Parker and they were the parents of four successful adults. He was a dedicated and active member of State Street Methodist Church. Jerry died January 19, 2007. Interment was in Fairview Cemetery.

Charles M. Moore, Jr.

Charles M. Moore (Charlie) Jr. was born March 16th, 1937. He resides with his wife of 51 years (his high school sweetheart) Shelby Greer Moore on Ewing Ford Road. They have three daughters. Charlie is Chairman of the Board of a large, four-generation, family-owned independent insurance agency. He has held numerous positions in the higher echelons of the insurance industry. He graduated from College High School. Charles has a Bachelors degree from the University of Kentucky and is a strong advocate for UK. His daughters are all UK graduates, and two of his nine grandchildren are now attending UK. Charlie joined Rotary in 1970 and served as president of the Bowling Green Club in 1979-1980. He is a Paul Harris Fellow and for many years has served the Club as Historian. He has been on and chaired many local civic organizations including the BG and Warren County Chamber of Commerce and the Warren County Chapter of Habitat for Humanity. He currently serves as Vice-Chairman of the Board of Commonwealth Health Foundation. Charlie has been and continues to be a great strength to the Bowling Green Rotary Club. He has been treasurer of Christ Episcopal Church for 50 years and continues in that service.

The Reverend Henry Howard Surface, Jr.

Howard Surface was born October 19, 1926 in Washington, D.C. He was educated in the District's public schools. He attended both Virginia Tech and Princeton University. He served in the U.S. Navy in World War II and was later commissioned Chaplain. His B.A. Degree was granted by the University of Virginia in 1948 and his Master of Divinity by Virginia Theological Seminary in 1951. He was ordained a deacon in 1951 and a priest in 1952. Reverend Surface was Associate Rector of St. Paul's Episcopal Church, Rock Creek Parish, Washington D.C. from 1951-1953. He was Rector of Christ Episcopal Church in Bowling Green, KY. from December 1953 until his retirement May 31, 1992. Howard has also served as Episcopal Chaplain at WKU and a founder and priest in charge of St. Andrews Episcopal Church in Glasgow, Kentucky.

On February 19,1954, Howard was married to Linda Anderson Smith of Georgetown, Kentucky. They have one adult son, David Howard Surface (WKU Bachelors Degree 1978) and one adult daughter, Mary Hall Surface (Outer College Bachelor's Degree 1980). Howard Surface joined Rotary in 1960 and has attended the weekly meetings for most of those fifty years. He frequently is asked to give the prayer at the weekly meetings.

At the Golden Anniversary of the Bowling Green Rotary club in 1970, Howard gave the invocation as he did at the 75th anniversary dinner in 1995. Howard Surface's caring nature has related well with the Rotary's motto of Service Above Self.

Col. Robert E. Spiller

Robert E. Spiller was born on Christmas Day in 1928. He is married to the former Cora Jane Morningstar and they reside in Oakland, Kentucky. Bob and Cora Jane are the parents of four children: Cora Jane, Robert, Nancy and Helen.

Bob had a distinguished military career rising to the rank of Colonel in the U.S. Army. His active duty career spanned three decades. Col. Spiller began his military career in 1950 and fought with the 25th Infantry in Korea and with the 1st Cavalry in Vietnam. During his career, he was stationed in France, Germany and the Pentagon, among other places. He is an enthusiastic supporter of the Salvation Army (rings the bells at Christmas). He renders financial support to Western Kentucky University, the Medical Center and the Girls Club. He supports the arts via the Bowling Green-Western Symphony Orchestra and Orchestra Kentucky.

Bob joined Rotary in 1980 where he has been tireless in his participation in Adopt-A-Class. He was on the organizing committee and serves as a mentor. He is a recipient of the Jefferson Award, as is his wife, Cora Jane, which was created in 1972 to honor the highest ideals and achievements in the field of Public Service. They both received this award in 2008. He is a docent at Riverview and the L. & N. Depot. He is volunteer organist at St. Andrews Episcopal Church in Glasgow and he and Cora Jane are members of Christ Episcopal Church in Bowling Green.

Colonel Spiller is a member of American Legion Post 23 and through this organization serves veterans in so many ways. He is totally dedicated to veterans services and is a strong advocate for veterans in all their needs, including Veterans Hospitals and Nursing Homes. Few Rotary meetings go by, in which Col. Spiller does not put in a good word for veterans. He is totally focused. He is a member of the VFW, is on the Joint Executive Council of Veterans Organization, meeting with the House and Senate as an advocate. No one in Rotary represents 'Service Above Self' more that Bob Spiller. Bob is a Paul Harris Fellow. The colonel was Grand Marshall of the local Veterans Parade on November 11, 2009.

Jody Richards

Jody Richards, who began his career on the faculty at Western Kentucky University, first ran for the Kentucky House of Representatives in 1975, at which time he won the 20th District House seat, an office he continues to hold. While still in his first term, Richards was appointed chair of the House Education Committee.

In 1987, Jody was chosen by his Democratic colleagues in the House to serve as their Majority Caucus Chairman, one of the chamber's five leadership positions. In 1995, he was elected Speaker of the House, a position he held until January of 2009. He is the longest-serving Speaker in Kentucky history. In 2003 and again in 2007, Rep. Richards was an unsuccessful candidate for the Democratic nomination for Kentucky governor.

Jody served as co-chair of one of three committees that wrote Kentucky's sweeping education reform in 1990 and helped to shepherd higher education reform through the legislature in 1997. In 2000, then- Speaker Richards sponsored a constitutional amendment and promoted passage by Kentucky voters to provide for annual sessions of the Kentucky General Assembly. It passed and the legislature began meeting in annual sessions in 2001.

Rep. Richards was elected Chair of the Southern Legislative conference in 1999 and continues to serve on the SLC Executive Committee. He has been on the Executive Committees of the National Conference of State Legislatures and the National Speakers Conference, on the Governing Board of the Council of State Governments, and is past chair of the Legislative Advisory Council of the Southern Regional Education Board.

In 2002, the Kentucky Rural Health Association and the Kentucky AARP both presented Rep. Richards with Outstanding Legislator of the Year Awards, and he was presented the co-legislator of the year award by the Kentucky League of Cities in 2008. He was the recipient of the William H. Natcher Award of Government Service and received the Hero Award from the Children's Advocacy Centers in 2000.

Jody has been a member of the Bowling Green Rotary Club since October 17, 1984.

John D. Minton

John D. Minton, Jr. was sworn in as the fifth Chief of Justice of Kentucky on June 27, 2008, after serving for two years as a Justice on the Supreme Court.

In November 2006, Chief Justice Minton was elected to an eight year term on the Supreme Court of Kentucky after running unopposed in the 2nd Supreme Court District, which is comprised of fourteen counties in western Kentucky. He first joined the Supreme Court in July 2006. when then–Governor Ernie Fletcher appointed him to fill the unexpired term created by the June 30, 2006, retirement of Justice William S. Cooper. Before sitting on the Supreme Court, Chief Justice Minton had been a Judge on the Kentucky Court of Appeals, the state's intermediate appellate court, beginning in November 2003.

Chief Justice Minton came to the appellate bench from the trial court. He was Judge of the Warren Circuit Court, Division 2, from 1992-2003. In addition to his trial court duties, he also served by special appointment of the late Chief Justice Robert F. Stephens and then-Chief Justice Joseph E. Lambert as Chief Administrative Judge of the Green River Region of Judicial Circuits, an administrative post assisting the Chief Justice with assigning special judges in a 21-county area of south central Kentucky.

While on the Circuit Court Bench, Chief Justice Minton was recognized for his leadership in forming Warren County Drug Court and for his commitment to law-related education programs. In 2003, the Kentucky Bar Association honored him with its Outstanding Judge Award. Chief Justice Minton was actively involved in continuing judicial education as a longtime member of the Education Committee of the Kentucky Circuit Judges Association.

Prior to his election to the circuit bench, Chief Justice Minton engaged in the private practice of law in Bowling Green, Kentucky for more than fifteen years. He graduated from the University of Kentucky College of Law in 1977 and was admitted to the Kentucky bar that same year. He earned his bachelor's degree with honors from Western Kentucky University in 1974 and is a 1970 graduate of Western Kentucky University High School (College High).

At a young age, Chief Justice Minton moved with his parents from Cadiz, Kentucky, to Bowling Green, where he grew up and currently resides. He is married to Susan Lenell Page, a Bowling Green native. The Minton's have two children, a daughter, Page Sullivan Minton, who is a sophomore at Washington and Lee University in Lexington, Virginia, and a son, John D. Minton, III, who is a high school junior.

Chief Justice Minton is the son of the late Dr. John D. Minton and Betty Redick Minton of Bowling Green. Dr. Minton, who passed away June 29, 2007, retired from Western Kentucky University, having served that institution for many years as history professor, administrator, and its fifth president. Mrs. Minton continues to live in Bowling Green.

John Minton became a member of the Bowling Green Rotary Club on May 5, 1993 and served as the club's President in 2001-2002.

Dan Cherry

United States Air Force Brigadier General Dan Cherry joined the Bowling Green Rotary Club in 1990. He had a distinguished career as a pilot of a F-4 in Southeast Asia.

The story that I want to relate, because it relates to Rotary in an oblique way, unfolded in 2009. In 2004, Dan and some friends visited the National Museum of the United States Air Force. They discovered that the very plane that Dan had been flying the day (4/16/1972) he shot down a North Vietnamese Mig and saw the pilot of that Mig eject and drift toward earth, was on static display at Dayton, Ohio. The plane was a F-4 #66-7550. The plane had suffered from the elements but otherwise was the same. After some discussions with the Air Force, a group of local Rotarians, namely, Carrol Hildreth, Kenneth Hines, Ward Coleman, and Hugh David Roe, came together and established Aviation Heritage Park, Inc. on Three Springs Road in Bowling Green. Money was raised and permission granted to move Phantom 550 for restoration and static display in Bowling Green.

A Vietnamese TV show began, named "The Separation that Never Seems to Have Existed." The show was able to locate the pilot of the Mig that Dan had shot down and an invitation was issued to both men to appear on the television show. Dan made the necessary inquiries and confirmations through the U.S. Embassy and was satisfied that it was all legitimate.

The two Air Force pilots, albeit, from opposing sides in the war, soon became comfortable with each other and while there Dan Cherry was invited to have dinner at Hong My's home where he met his family. The trip and the encounter had gone well.

In the Spring of 2009, Hong My was invited to visit Dan Cherry in Bowling Green, where Dan brought him as a guest to Rotary. There was much sight-seeing in the United States, as there had been in Hanoi. While in Bowling Green there was a visit to the Aviation Park to view the restored F4D. There were visits to the nation's capitol and joint appearances on national television. Dan has since published a book called "My Enemy, My Friend". The entire story is interesting reading for Rotarians and indeed for Americans of all walks of life.

Vickie Elrod

Vickie Elrod was born November 20, 1950. She is currently employed by Holland and Associates CPAs where she is Chief Operating Officer, as well as Human Resources Consultant. She provides Human Resources Consulting to her firm, as well as, to small business clients. Previously, she spent twenty years in the banking industry. Vickie is the wife of Robert Elrod and they have four children.

Vickie was one of the earliest women members of the Bowling Green Rotary Club, joining in 1991. She has been a very active member, serving as President in 2005-2006. She is a Paul Harris Fellow and a sustaining member. She has also shown a great interested in District 6710 affairs and presently serves as an Assistant District Governor. She is involved in many civic organizations and a dedicated member of her church – First Baptist – where she sings in the choir.

Her hobbies are mostly outdoor activities but are balanced with cross stitching, photography and scrapbooking.

Margaret Curtis

Margaret Curtis joined the Bowling Green Rotary Club in 1996. She is a Paul Harris Fellow, level three.

Margaret maintains that she was "raised underneath the streets of London" during World War II. This statement is not far from the truth! Her family eventually moved north to Warwickshire, and she completed her higher education at the Universities of Sheffield, London and Manchester.

Eventually the United Kingdom felt too restricting (i.e. no jobs) so she emigrated to Canada in 1969, and then to Kentucky in 1972. She was appointed to a position in the Philosophy and Religion Department at Western Kentucky University, where she remained until her retirement in 2000. She taught Greek, Religious Studies, and Middle Eastern Studies.

Throughout her teaching career Margaret traveled widely in Europe and in the Middle East. She taught American Literature during a Fulbright Year at Sana's University, Yemen, and she traveled widely through Egypt, Israel, Jordan, Syria and Turkey. Margaret also spent time in South America – Ecuador and Argentina. After retirement she turned her attention to Asia – Thailand, Singapore and China. In China she taught Western Cultures and Spoken English at Chongqing Technical and Business University, 2008-2009.

Margaret never won an award for perfect attendance and was never invited to join the Club board. However, she was active as a member of the Rotary Travel and Hosting Fellowship, the Rotary RV Fellowship and Rotary Volunteers. In the latter capacity she served as a Rotary Volunteer teaching English in Kocaeli-Golcuk, Turkey, July 2007. This project was celebrated in the April 2009 volume of "Rotary World."

District Governors

The Bowling Green Rotary Club in its almost ninety years has produced six District Governors. They were William J. Craig, J. Murray Hill, Sr., William L. Matthews, Dr. Walter J. Munday, Dr. Ward Sumpter and William J. (Jerry) Parker. J. Murray Hill, Sr. also attained the highest office of any Bowling Green Rotary Club member when he served as Director of Rotary International and was twice sent by Rotary as a representative to international meetings in Europe and Asia.

Documents

1920

INTERNATIONAL ASSOCIATION
OF
ROTARY CLUBS

HEADQUARTERS 910 SOUTH MICHIGAN AVENUE, CHICAGO, U.S.A.

OFFICE OF THE SECRETARY
EXECUTIVE DEPARTMENT

17 August, 1920
File 300-Bowling Green, Ky.

Dr. E. D. Rose
Bowling Green, Ky.

My dear Mr. Rose:

Our President, Estes Snedecor, has appointed you chairman of the Organizing Committee for the Rotary Club of Bowling Green, with authority to select the members of your committee.

District Governor Chas. W. Bailey has asked us to send you some Rotary literature and to supplement his letters of instruction with some from this office. The enclosed "Manual of Information for Chairmen of Organizing Committees of Rotary Clubs" will give you complete instructions as to how to proceed. Study Pamphlet No. 10 over carefully. The information contained in this manual is a compilation based upon the work in organizing the seven hundred sixty and more Rotary Clubs now in existence. We have found that any organizing committee which will follow the instructions of the manual will build up a successful Rotary Club.

There is an affiliation fee for clubs charged on the basis of one dollar for every thousand population in the city where the club is located, but such affiliation fee shall not be less than a minimum of twenty-five dollars nor more than a maximum of one hundred dollars.

This affiliation fee must accompany the application for affiliation.

The expenses of the district governor in attending the institutional meeting will be paid by the Association.

The Board of Directors of the International Association has ruled that the charter membership list of each Rotary Club hereafter organized shall be comprised of not less than fifteen, nor more than twenty-five classifications, and that the list of members submitted to the Association as part of the application for affiliation shall be the club's charter membership list and that, pending action of the Board of Directors of the Association on the application, no other members shall be elected to the club.

September 1st, 1920.

The present charter members of the Rotary Club of Bowling Green, Kentucky, met September 1, 1920, in the Assembly Room of the Farm Bureau. Doctor Ed Rose the authorized organizer presided until the permanent organization was effected with W. J. Craig acting as Secretary. Constitution and By Laws were adopted, a copy of which is herewith appended to this minute. The body then elected an executive committee consisting of the following members: J. Whit Potter, J. O. Carson, W. J. Craig, F. D. Cartwright and A. S. Hines. This committee then went into immediate session and elected the following permanent officers: J. Whit Potter, president, J. O. Carson, vice president, W. J. Craig, secretary, Harold Sublett, treasurer, and E. B. Stout sargeant at arms. By motion the entertainment committee was instructed to provided for a special meeting to be held in Bowling Green, September 16th at which meeting District Governor C. W. Bailey, and other Rotarians were to be invited. President then appointed the following committees: Entertainment committee, F. B. Stout, J. Mott Williams and Guy Jones; Membership committee, J. O. Carson, Guy Herdman, F. D. Cartwright, Sam Crystal and G. P. Evans. The house then adjourned by motion.

J. Whit Potter
President.

W. J. Craig
Secretary.

January 25, 1922.

The Bowling Green Rotary Club met in regular session in the dining room of the First Presbyterian Church. Lunch was served and the house called to order by President, J. Whit Potter. Roll was called and the minutes for the two previous meetings were read and adopted. The club sang "America" lead by Rotarian Bill Hill.

A visitor, J. C. Hall, of Louisville, Ky. made a pleasant little greeting to the club. Secretary was instructed to write to the speaker of our social meeting and thank him for his scholarly address.

Adjourned by the chair.

Number of members present 33. Percent of attendance 94%.

J. Whit Potter
President.

W. J. Craig
Secretary.

A MODEL CHARTER MEMBERSHIP LIST

CHARTER MEMBERSHIP LIST MUST ACCOMPANY APPLICATION FOR AFFILIATION

ROTARY CLUB OF BOWLING GREEN, KENTUCKY.

ROSTER LIST OF CHARTER MEMBERSHIP

Closed September 1, 1920.

he Secretary of the

national Association of Rotary Clubs,
910 Michigan Avenue, Chicago, U. S. A.

District Governor's Office.)

The following have been duly elected to and have accepted membership

Rotary Club of Bowling Green, Kentucky:

Carson, Dr. J. O.
Physician, Eye, Ear, Nose, and Throat
442 1/2 Main Street, BOWLING GREEN, KENTUCKY
Res. address, 1133 State Street.

Cartwright, Dr. F. D.
Physician, General Practice
Corner Tenth and State Streets, BOWLING GREEN, KENTUCKY
Res. address, Foster Apartments.

Craig, W. J.
Teacher, Head Department of Science,
Western Kentucky State Normal School, BOWLING GREEN, KENTUCKY
Res. address, R. R. No. 4.

Cuthbertson, Sterrett
Retail Dry Goods, Joseph Cuthbertson Company
478 Main Street, BOWLING GREEN, KENTUCKY
Res. address, 633 East Main Street.

Crystal, Sam
Produce Dealer, Partner in Sam Nahm Company
823 State Street, BOWLING GREEN, KENTUCKY
Res. address, 618 Main Street.

Evans, G. P.
Division Superintendent Postal Service.
(Under Civil Service.)
Post Office, BOWLING GREEN, KENTUCKY
Res. address, 316 Tenth Street.

--2--

Herdman, Guy
Lawyer, Herdman and Roper
Neale Building, BOWLING GREEN, KENTUCKY
Res. address, 640 Main Street.

Hines, A. S.
Wholesale Grocer, Supt. Parson-Scoville Company
Cor. Kentucky and Main Streets, BOWLING GREEN, KENTUCKY
Res. address, cor. Main and Elm Streets.

Jones, Gus S.
Tobacco Dealer, Tobacco Factory
666 Adams Street, BOWLING GREEN, KENTUCKY
Res. address cor. Fifteenth and College Streets.

Potter, J. Whit
Banker, President American National Bank
922 State Street, BOWLING GREEN, KENTUCKY
Res. address, St. James Apartments.

Rose, Dr. E. D.
Dentist,
Office 914 1/2 State Street, BOWLING GREEN, KENTUCKY
Res. address, 1415 College Street.

Stout, E. B.
Real Estate Dealer, Stout and Cook
321 Main Street, BOWLING GREEN, KENTUCKY
Res. address, 1332 Park Street.

Sublett, Harold W.
Druggist, Partner in Carpenter-Dent-Sublett Co.
Cor. College Street and Park Row, BOWLING GREEN, KENTUCKY
Res. address, 1019 Center Street.

Warrener, S. K.
Livestock Breeder, Registered sheep and cattle
Res. and business address, Boatlanding Pike, BOWLING GREEN, KENTUCKY

Williams, J. Mott
Retail Clothing for Men, Williams--Moore Company
908 State Street, BOWLING GREEN, KENTUCKY
Res. address, 1303 State Street.

October 2, 1923

Mr. John D. Taylor, Sec.,
Rotary Club,
Bristol,
Virginia.

Dear Joe:

Herewith I am enclosing according to our agreement copy of the monthly attendance for the Bowling Green Rotary Club.

We worked rather hard on this attendance, and I hope we have beaten you.

I also hope that you, too, have worked hard, and have made a splendid attendance.

With best wishes for you and your boys, I remain

Most sincerely,

        Secretary.

WJC:Els

W J Craig

THE PINION

The Weekly Bulletin of The Bowling Green Rotary Club

Vol. I.   July 13, 1925   No. 11.

REGULAR WEEKLY MEETING - - HELM HOTEL, WEDNESDAY NOON.

The meeting on Wednesday will be in charge of the Committee on Public affairs, ow which Doc. Riggs is Chairman. Every Rotarian should be present as Doc. is sure to put on something good.

--- oOo ---

DID YOU KNOW

That after all bills had been paid, and the accounts audited, after the District Conference in March, held in Louisville, the committee in charge found a balance of $1,074.07 in the Treasury, which was divided as follows:

One-third to the Tennessee Society for Crippled Children.
One-third to the Kentucky Society for Crippled Children.
One-third to the Boys' Work Committee of the Rotary Club of Louisville.

--- oOo ---

You will be glad to know that Rotarian Guy H. Herdman is continuing to improve and that the doctors say that it will not be so very long before he will be with us again.

--- oOo ---

Rotarian Alex N. Taylor, Secretary of the Rotary Club at Henderson, Ky., writes the following "Philosophy of Life."

"Did it ever occur to you that a man's life is full of crosses and temptations? He comes into the world without his consent and goes out of it against his will, and the trip between is exceedingly rocky. The rule of contraries is one of the features of the trip.

"When he is little, the big girls kiss him; when he is big, the little girls kiss him.
"If he is poor, he is a bad manager; if he is rich, he is dishonest.
"If he needs credit, he can't get it; if he is prosperous, every one wants to do him a favor.
"If he is in politics, it is for graft; if he is out of politics, he is no good to his country.
"If he doesn't give to charity, he is a stingy cuss; if he does, it is for show.
"If he is actively religious, he is a hypocrite; if he takes no interest in religion, he is a hardened sinner.
"If he gives affection, he is a soft specimen; if he cares for no one, he is cold-blooded.
"If he dies young, there was a great future before him; if he lives to an old age, he missed his calling.
"If you save money, you're a grouch; if you spend it, you're a loafer;
"If you get it, you're a grafter; if you can't get it, you're a bum
          So what the H---'s the use."

ABSENTEES:

aft. June 1927

TO THE MEMBERS OF THE BOWLING GREEN ROTARY CLUB:

THIS RECOMMENDATION, respectfully submitted by the Boys' Work Committee, O. V. Clark, Chairman, that the following buildings be authorized by the Club:

Four huts to accommodate eight boys each, one building twenty feet by fifty feet for dining room and kitchen, and two toilets. Also, a fence to be built at the top of the hill to keep cattle out. The estimated cost of this work and possibly a few minor repairs will be approximately $600.00.

It is also recommended that the Committee be authorized to employ Jack Smith, if it is possible to do so, to have charge of the camp during the summer months, and it is understood that he will charge $25.00 per week for his services. This, however, will be paid for in part, or possibly in full, by the boys attending the camp, as an extra amount will be charged to their expenses over and above the necessary expenses for their cook and meals to cover a part, and possibly all, of Mr. Smith's or someone's else services.

It is also recommended that the Committee have full authority with reference to allowing anyone the privilege of going to the camp, and that the program will be worked out in co-operation with the Boy Scout movement and the Y. M. C. A.

It is also recommended that two weeks during the summer months, dates to be arranged when the program is worked out, be set aside for the use of the Rotary members, provided any of them care to take advantage of the camp life. When these two weeks are set apart, it will be announced, and it will be necessary for any members desiring to use the camp to notify the Chairman in charge two weeks in advance of the time that they desire to use it.

It is further recommended that in case none of the members of the club desire to take advantage of the camp during the weeks set apart, the committee will have the privilege to allow someone else the privilege of the camp during this time.

Summing up the recommendation, the Committee wishes the Club to authorize the expenditure of $600.00 on improvements, and the authority to hire Jack Smith, if possible, to look after the property during the summer months, and, in case his services can not be had, that they be authorized to employ the services of someone else whom they consider capable.

Respectfully submitted,

BOYS' WORK COMMITTEE,

STATEMENT

Bowling Green, Ky., 12/28 193 8

M Rotary Club

IN ACCOUNT WITH

HELM HOTEL

ACCOUNTS DUE WHEN PRESENTED

ROOM							
47	Plate 50¢			$23	50		
	Paid 1/10/39						
	Ck #1437						
			TOTAL	$23	50		

RECEIVED PAYMENT, HELM HOTEL

Per ....

Note how much cheaper the meals were— only 50¢ per plate in 1938!

OFFICIAL PROGRAM and RULES

Governing

1940 Hobby Fair

Sponsored By The

Bowling Green Rotary Club

President, Top Orendorf
Sec.-Treas., Sam Cooke

TIME—May 3 and 4, 1940, Bowling Green, Ky.
PLACE—Former A&P Location...Park Row

Every girl and boy in Warren County is urged to select a Hobby that may be pursued during leisure time from which pleasure and profit will come.

Definitions and Rules

Judging between one and five Saturday afternoon.

Trophies and medals awarded on basis of: Neatness of booth, decorations, knowledge of subject, skill, contents of booth.

Two must be in all booths working at all times, while show is open.

Prizes

First Prize .... GRAND TROPHY
Outstanding City Hobby .... TROPHY
Outstanding County Hobby .... TROPHY

Medals and Ribbons for Participants in Outstanding Booths

HOBBY SHOW COMMITTEE

Dr. Wallace Barr
R. M. Parrish
Harry Biggs
Robert A. Smith, Chairman

1920-1929

Bowling Green Rotary Club founded

Early members and meeting place

Charter presented

At least through 1923 maintained atendence record of 96%

Purchased Boy Scout Camp and grounds on Drakes Creek

First committee for Crippled Children's work

First clinic for the above

Raised money to rebuild nine-mile section of cobblestone road south of Patk City, KY

Willaim J. Craig- District Governor

Weekly bulletin "The Pinion"

10¢ fine for calling anyone by other than his given name or nick-name

1930-1939

Eugene Newson visits Bowling Green

Contests with Glasgow club

Assisted in organizing Cave City Club

Promoted service to country schools

Emory Dent Bridge

Cemetery Pike

Murray Hill, Sr. was a director of Rotary International

Promotion of Mammoth Cave Natioanl Park

Organization of Scottesville club

Lewie Harman visited President Coolidge

Old Drakes Creek Camp sold, New property purchased

Murray Hill and W. J. Mathews attended R.I. convention in France

Marray Hill, Sr. was District Governor

30's continued

W. L. Mathews was District Governor

Rotoscript

College Day held

1940-1949

Activity at Rotary Camp for Scouts

Many programs of military emphasis

Crippled children's work continued

War Bonds sales drive (tremendous success)

Contributions to War Fund, community Chest, Christmas expense for servicemen visiting B.G. canteen

Victory Garden Contest promotion

Rotary Camp sold

Contributions to hospital

A Barter Theatre production of Hamlet was sponsored to raise money for the Delafield School

1950-1959

Delafield School milk fund program

Boys State delegate

Little Baseball Program

Irish girl at Western under Rotary sponsorship

Attention drawn to 31-W

Annual Country Ham Show

Heart Fund

1960-1969

Swedish Girl at Western under Rotary sponsorship

Donation to Camp KYSOC

Ward Sumpter was District Governor

"The Cog"

Hobby Fair (big event-almost 100% participation)

Asphalting playground area for Salvation Army

Jerry Hornback-Rotary Foundation Fellow studying in Ireland

Rummage Sale to raise money for Camp KYSOC

Fireside Chats

1970-1979

Steve Smith studied in England as Rotary Scholar

50th anniversary celebration

Money to city schools for shoes, clothing, and books, during exceptionally hard winter

Second club in district to participate 100% in Health, Hunger, and Humanity program

Tom Hall- Paul Harris Fellow

HELP! I'm lacking information form the 70's! What programs has Rotary been involved in?

Maharaja Contest 4 times in 70's avge $2000.00

Pledge to flag during 70's

contribution to College Heights Foundation 3 W.K.U. students each fall - local High Schools

Camp

WS, BOWLING GREEN, KY.

To The B.G. Rotary Club

Being sick and unable to attend a meeting
I have decided to write you this greeting,
And as my ears sing all the time,
It is easiest for me to write in rhyme.
I am neither a Byron, Shelley nor Keats,
Nor inclined to do poetical feats,
But when I'm at home, sick in bed,
And the poetical bee buzzing in my head,
It is hard for me to stay right still
And not fly my Pegasus on Reservoir Hill.

I can see John Tyler, our president,
Shooting his darts of merriment.
When John takes a crack, you'd better duck low,
For when he turns loose, away they go.
He lets them fly, whatever the occasion,
And don't give a d—— who feels the abrasion.
John started in Rotary as a Coca-Cola shark,
But he soon shed his mantle on O. V. Clark.
He then took up the "Capitalist Class,"
But bankers got jealous, so he had to pass.
He then resorted to building the chest
In which dead men's bones are laid to rest.
He had a fire, but it didn't faze John,
For it gave him an idea to work upon.
He now lines his coffins with an asbestos roof
And guarantees the market they're "hell-fire proof."

Since Scott and Bill Sumpter seem to be
Rival candidates for the mayoralty,
And the political bee is buzzing in each,
And both have the plum within their reach,
Suppose the Rotary Club settle this race
By electing both to Mayor Stone's place.
As the term's four years, it's easy to fill,
Give Scott two years, and the rest to Bill.

Do you ever hear now from old Murray Hill?
His and Harmon's places are hard to fill.
They are certainly well mated in the old B. U.,
And also in the Rotary Club, too.
For when one talks out, the other takes his place.
They really are best in a relay race
And the good thing about it, it is easy for each
To give the club at any time a prepared impromptu speech.

There is one thing certain, and I'm sure you don't know it,
But Dr. Jim Carson is certainly some poet.
He once wrote a sonnet, or perhaps you'd say an ode,
And he wrote it up in Bret Harte's code.
He took as his theme, "Love's Sweet Cup,"
At a fair hop he went to when Hector was a pup.
He filled his verses with sweet-scented tresses,
Heaving bosoms and tender caresses.
In fact, Bill Schell, who now hand the dope,
Should have Doctor Carson walk his poetry rope.
If he's too timid to read his turn,
There'd be no reluctance, if he asked Guy Byrn.

There's another member, and he's Ed Stout,
If he is my cousin, he's a good old scout

This poem was in an envelope with this written explanation by Ward Sumpter: "EB Stout Sr. was a charter member altho not listed in JL Harman's 1955 History. Guy Herdman was the father of Asst. Atty Gen. Herdman. John Tyler father of Sarah Tyler. O.V. Clarke the father of O.V. Jr. Roland Fitch was the father of Roland Jr., late pres. of BG Trust. The date of the Poem was 1925 as evidenced by the election comments."

BOWLING GREEN ROTARY CLUB

OFFICERS
J. R. MEANY
President
GEORGE H. MOSELEY
Vice President
SAMUEL C. COOKE
Secretary-Treasurer

"SERVICE ABOVE SELF"

HE PROFITS MOST WHO SERVES BEST"

DIRECTORS
J. R. MEANY
GEORGE H. MOSELEY
E. WALLACE BARR
EMORY G. DENT
J. MURRAY HILL
L. T. SMITH

BOWLING GREEN, KENTUCKY

October 11, 1933

TO THE BOWLING GREEN ROTARY CLUB:

Your Committee, set up to submit to you some major activities for the present Rotary year, from which list you might make your choice, offers the following report:

Public interest in a city the size of Bowling Green includes CHURCHES SCHOOLS, MORALS, BEAUTY, ROADS, STREETS, HEALTH, CHARITY PARKS, PLAYGROUND

From these interests your committee made a list of sixteen subjects given here but no in the order of their importance:

GENERAL LIST

1. Back-to-school Movement
2. More attention to Crippled Children
3. Assist the Mammoth Cave National Park Commission and the Mammoth Cave National Park Association in completing the task of turning the Park Area over to the Government.
4. Advertise the attractive features of Bowling Green to the tourists who pass through here.
5. A Home-coming day for former Bowling Green Boys.
6. Endeavor to induce the State Highway Dept to rebuild the Dixie Highway from Horse Cave to Munfordville.
7. Endeavor to secure a City Manager form of Government for Bowling Green.
8. Establish more intimate relationships between the citizens and the college students of Bowling Green.
9. Promote a College Day.
10. Systematic promotion of a Rotary School.
11. More beauty and cleanliness in our City.
12. A continuous interest and activity in the Welfare Home.
13. More attention to the blind of Warren County.
14. An airport for Bowling Green.
15. More attention to Boys' Work.

BOWLING GREEN ROTARY CLUB

"SERVICE ABOVE SELF"

"HE PROFITS MOST WHO SERVES BEST"

BOWLING GREEN, KENTUCKY

September 10, 1941.

TO MEMBERS OF ROTARY CLUB:

At our last meeting a proposal was made that the Bowling Green Rotary Club underwrite $1000 of the sum necessary to acquire the land for a Bowling Green Airport.

By vote of the Club the matter was referred to the Board. After considerable discussion the Board declined to take action until it knew the full sentiment of the Club.

To this end the Board requests that you please check the enclosed card and mail at once, without signature.

Sincerely yours,

S. C. Cooke

S. C. Cooke, Secretary

SCC:SG

J. MURRAY HILL, PRESIDENT   W. L. MATTHEWS, VICE PRESIDENT

BOWLING GREEN COLLEGE OF COMMERCE
INCORPORATED
SENIOR COLLEGE--A-RATING
DIVISION OF
BOWLING GREEN BUSINESS UNIVERSITY

COURSES OF STUDY:
COMMERCIAL TEACHER TRAINING
ACCOUNTING
BUSINESS ADMINISTRATION
COLLEGE SECRETARIAL

MEMBER KENTUCKY ASSOCIATION OF
COLLEGES AND SECONDARY SCHOOLS

BOWLING GREEN, KY.
November 6, 1957

TO THE ROTARY CLUB:

    Many times the spirit and words of Rotary have been encouraging to me, but at no time more meaningful than in my recent great sorrow. Your flowers sent while Mrs. Harman was ill, your elaborate floral design of last week, your presence in our home, your handgrasps, your words, letters and cards give me anew the high worth and spirit of Rotary.

    For your kindness and sympathy, Lewie, Jr., and I thank you.

J. L. Harman

HONORING 75 YEARS

MEMBERSHIP IN ROTARY INTERNATIONAL

The Rotary Club of

Bowling Green, Kentucky, USA

admitted 1 November 1920

is recognized for its dedication
to the Object of Rotary and its commitment
to the ideal of Service Above Self.

Herbert G. Brown   1 November 1995   _[signature]_
President, Rotary International   Date   General Secretary, Rotary International

---

Chronology from *Western Kentucky University,* 1987, Dr. Lowell H. Harrison.

1906-1922 Western Kentucky State Normal[1] School
1922-1930 Western Kentucky State Normal School and Teachers College
1930-1948 Western Kentucky State Teachers College
1948-1966 Western Kentucky State College
1966-Present Western Kentucky University

Presidents of Western:
Henry Hardin Cherry   Donald W. Zacharias
Paul L. Garrett   Paul B. Cook (interim)
Kelly Thompson   Kern Alexander
Dero G. Downing   Thomas Meredith
John D. Minton, Sr.   Gary Ransdell

[1] Normal Schools were for training teachers.

The Press

MARVIN BROWN
Joined Rotary 1942

BILL BROWN
Joined Rotary 1969

The Browns

Both Rotarians and owners of Brown Ice Cream Company later called Browns Dairy Foods

Cooke's Hand Records Club

Samuel Coombs Cooke, who joined the Bowling Green Rotary Club in 1924, serves as the organization's secretary, an office he has held for 45 years.

Joining the club in July, 1924, Cooke began serving as secretary in July, '925, a year after he joined the organization.

Born June 1, 1895, in Bowling Green, Cooke served with the U. S. Army during World War I. Ten months of his two years of service then were spent in France.

Active in church and civic affairs, he is an elder in the Bowling Green Presbyterian Church.

Married to the former Miss Elsie Burmeister, Cooke and his wife have two sons, Sam C. Cooke Jr. and Raymond B. Cooke.

The late Paul L. Garrett often referred to Cooke as the "family man of Rotary" because of the many hours Cooke spent with his sons.

Cooke has served 45 years as club secretary and has been attested by 45 presidents of the Bowling Green Rotary Club and district governors of Rotary International.

Cooke often has been praised by his club for making reports on time, in full detail and acccurately.

Clubs Urged To Discuss World Problems

William E. Walk Jr., president of Rotary International this year urges each Rotary club to make its club a forum for a complete and open discussion for the world's ever growing problems.

Listing the problems as the need for bridges between people, nations and man and his environment, Walk urged clubs to "support agencies designed to bridge the gap in our societies. If such agencies do not exist, take the leadership yourself to enlighten, to help find the answers and in help solve these problem.

SAMUEL C. COOKE

ROTARY FOUNDING 31 YEARS AGO IS OBSERVED TODAY

Local Club Hears Emory G. Dent In Interesting Address

The thirty-first anniversary of the founding of Rotary International was observed at today's meeting of the local club, with Emory G. Dent as speaker.

Mr. Dent reviewed the growth and development of Rotary from its beginning to date, devoting half of his time to remarks concerning the organization as a whole and the remainder to the local club. In an interesting manner the speaker described the beginning of Rotary in Chicago in 1905 and traced its growth to the present time—an organization with more than 150,000 members of its 3,600 clubs in 80 countries of the world.

Mr. Dent paid a high tribute to several of the past presidents of the local club, organized in 1920. He also mentioned the fame the local club has attained because of its distinguished members, J. Murray Hill, of the board of directors of Rotary International, and the late General William L. Sibert, an honorary member.

Because of the occasion several former Rotarians were guests of the club today. They were Dr. J. O.

Daily News, 7-26-1936

ROTARIANS
'S LOCAL CLUB

March 20, 1930

In the center of the dance floor is a pool from which a bathing girl or water nymph will entertain the guests while young women from the Western State Normal will render folk-dances and sing songs during the luncheon hour.

About the hall are palms and blooming plants of various kinds direct from the hot houses. Beneath the balcony are rows of tables where the guests will be served a luncheon by the ladies of Christ Episcopal church.

International President Eugene Newson, of Durham, N. C., will be the guest of honor and will make the principal address of the evening. He will be introduced by former District Governor Coleman Taylor, of Russellville. President P. C. Deemer of the local Rotary club will preside as toastmaster. Addresses will be made by other local and visiting Rotarians.

Following the luncheon and other entertainments for the visitors a dance will follow.

Visitors from clubs at Louisville, Ashland, Eminence, Lebanon, Fulton, Auburn, Russellville, Elkton, Hopkinsville, Henderson, Owensboro, Franklin, Glasgow, Nashville, Springfield, Tenn., and other cities will be present and in all some four hundred and fifty are expected to be present at the festivities tonight.

It will be the most elaborate entertainment both in point of decorations and visitors ever gathered in the portals of the city and will be an occasion long to be remembered by not only Rotarians but citizens as well. The guest list will include Rotarians, their wives and invited guests.

COLLEGE DAY TO BE NOTED HERE IN MAY

(Continued from Page One)

hours. The expenses of the day's entertainment will be borne by local citizens.

The College Day idea was proposed some time ago and met with instant response wherever discussed. The latter part of May was designated as that is the time for commencement activities at the two colleges and the program will constitute a farewell party to the students.

Schools City's Chief Industry

George H. Moseley, who presided at last night's committee meeting, described Bowling Green's two great institutions as the leading industry of the city and an industry which did not suffer greatly during the depression. He said that money spent locally as a result of the schools' operation during the past few years meant much in keeping Bowling Green "above the average" of business conditions prevailing in less fortunate towns.

He stated Bowling Green is a college town and appreciates the schools but has never had opportunity to show this appreciation in a tangible way. The observance of College Day, which it is hoped will be an annual affair, will afford such an opportunity, he said.

Sterret Cuthbertson, local banker and member of the Board of Regents of the Western Teachers College, also spoke enthusiastically concerning the proposal. He stated Western Teachers College is now the largest teachers college in the world, without exception, and that the Bowling Green Business University is the largest institution of its type in America.

Other talks were made at the session last night by W. C. Sumpter, J. L. Harman, T. M. Hunt and Sam Pushin.

Those present at the meeting as representatives of various local organizations and city departments were: W. C. Sumpter, L. T. Smith, B. S. Rutherford, J. Q. Kirby, Earl D. Rabold, Hubert Devasier, George Donnelly, John Davis, Charles Long, Weldon Peete, Alvis Temple, Tom Morris Hunt, Sam Pushin, J. P. Masters, Sterret Cuthbertson, J. L. Harman, W. H. Arnold, George H. Moseley and Sam C. Cooke.

Part of Cemetery Road

BE IT RESOLVED BY THE BOWLING GREEN ROTARY CLUB, INCORPORATED: That whereas there are 7.2 miles of unimproved road on what is known as the Bowling Green-Claypool highway and also known as State Project 142, and whereas said road leads from Bowling Green, Kentucky to Claypool, thence to Meador, Gainesville and Scottsville, Kentucky, and whereas said road has been under construction for many years and only 7.2 miles are unimproved, and whereas said road is of great economic and commercial value to Warren and Allen Counties and Bowling Green and Scottsville, Kentucky, and whereas a bus line now travels said road, and whereas the cost of the right-of-way has been obtained free of cost to the state and primarily at the cost of the property-owners along said highway, and whereas the completion of said project has been tentatively promised for several years,

NOW, THEREFORE, BE IT RESOLVED BY THE BOWLING GREEN ROTARY CLUB, INCORPORATED that the State Highway Department be requested to take immediate steps to complete said road and if possible give said construction priority, thereby completing the only important, unimproved road leading out of Bowling Green. AND BE IT FURTHER RESOLVED that a copy of this resolution be sent to John A. Keck, Highway Commissioner of Frankfort, Kentucky, and a copy be sent to LaMar Riney, District Engineer of Bowling Green, Kentucky.

------------------------------- PRESIDENT

-------------------------------SECRETARY

COLLEGE DAY

NEWSPAPER OF MAY 24, 1934

"The 3200 students of the Western Kentucky State College and the Bowling Green Business University marched to Fountain Square Park where they were met by citizens in automobiles and conveyed to the city's new park in Covington Woods. There they enjoyed an excellent program followed by serving an old-fashion barbecue supper. The day's program was completed with a theatre party during which students and teachers were admitted free to the Capitol and Diamond Theatres.

"About 4000 persons were served at supper.

"The junior class of each college was awarded a silver plaque for having presented the best stunt from its college.

"One of the stunts was a take-off on the Common Council of Bowling Green in which the students depicted a session of the Council during the late Ducks-Scout dispute.

* * * * * *

"Before the students program, talks were made by Judge John B. Rodes, Dr. B. S. Rutherford, Mayor, Dr. H. H. Cherry, President of Western, and Dr. J. L. Harman, President, Business University.

"Moving pictures of the parade were made from a specially constructed stand at Tenth and College Streets by a camera-man brought here through the interest of Col. John P. Masters of the Crescent Amusement Company.

"Other shots taken at the park included the preparation of the barbecue and interesting parts of the afternoon program. The pictures will be shown at the Capitol next week.

"Police and deputy sheriffs cooperated in controlling traffic and the task of moving the huge crowd was accomplished without an accident.

"Pres. Cherry, Pres. Harman, and Vice-Pres. J. Murray Hill said they appreciated this civic demonstration more than anything that has ever happened in the life of the schools."

Newspaper articles regarding College Day, held May 24, 1934

The Laying of the Cornerstone

This day is outstanding in the life of College Heights -
a day of which many of us have dreamed -
a day that is conspicuous and prophetic in the life of
Western, as we meet to lay the cornerstone of a
building, representative alike of the need of the hour
and the hope of the future.
As this great classroom structure takes its place upon the Hill, those of
the present strive earnestly to build worthily and
adequately for the future.
In laying the cornerstone of this noble building,
dedicated to service and democracy, we pray that it may arise, not
only to the splendid proportion of its architectural plans
but that it may become symbolic of the urgent need of a broader,
a more vigorous and varied preparation,
of the thousands of young men and women who shall pass through its
portals, who shall cast their armour here, in which they will go forth to
meet the responsibilities, the opportunities and
the conflicts of a swiftly moving era.
With our eyes upon a goal that reaches into the future, we are charting
a program of action that calls for the same spirit, devotion, and
support that brought the institution to the achievement of this hour.
With a spirit of gratitude, humility, and of rising faith
we re-dedicate our lives to the work of the future,
to the growing of a great Western.

President Henry Hardin Cherry
October 27, 1936
Dedication of New Classroom and Laboratory Building
Western Kentucky Teachers College
Bowling Green, Kentucky

(known today as Cherry Hall)

Rotarians Entertain With Christmas Party

Dec. 23, 1953

Rotarians today entertained their children with a Christmas party in the main dining room of the Helm Hotel.

About 200 Rotarians and guests attended the luncheon, which was featured by a visit from Santa Claus.

Earliest reference to Christmas Party for Children as occurs in 2009 format was 1936. Before that, there were father-son or -daughter dinners near Christmas.

Article from the Daily News, dated 1953

Articles dated 12-5-1938

The Captain's Party
BOWLING GREEN, KY.

Host: Capt. and Mrs. Walter G. Hougland
Guest: Members of Bowling Green Rotary Club and their Ladies.

HELM HOTEL   DEC. 5, 1938

Captain Hougland Is Host To Members Of Rotary Club Here

12/5/38

Approximately 125 Rotarians, their wives and guests, were entertained by Captain and Mrs. Walter G. Hougland of Owensboro with a dinner last night at the Helm hotel.

Although Captain Hougland, prominent riverman who formerly resided here and was a member of the local Rotary club, was the host at the dinner, the program was arranged by local Rotarians as a surprise.

The theme of the program was "Steamboat on the River," and the hotel dining room was appropriately decorated with miniature river boats, lifeboats, and lighthouses. The menu also carried out the boat scheme with various delicacies named after the boats in the Hougland fleet.

R. Douglas Willock, president of the Rotary club, served as "pilot" during the program. Mr. Willock introduced each speaker with a rhyme. The speakers spoke on the various stages of a boat trip. Paul L. Garrett spoke on "Shoving Off," W. J. Craig on "The Voyage," and L. B. Finn on "The Landing." W. L. Matthews concluded the program with "Hail to the Captain." Captain Hougland was called upon for a short talk at the conclusion of the evening.

Music throughout the program was rendered by the Jubilee Singers of Fisk University, Nashville. The singers rendered several river songs.

In addition to Captain and Mrs. Hougland, other special guests at the dinner were Captain and Mrs. James Hougland of Calhoun and Mrs. Robert Hougland of Calhoun, Mrs. Glover Cary and Mr. and Mrs. Walter Hougland, Jr., of Owensboro, and Mr. and Mrs. Edwin Burton and Mrs. Nola Shutt of this city.

Rotary International President To Talk Here

Tom Warren   **Joseph MacPherson**

Plans have been completed by the Bowling Green Rotary Club to honor T. A. "Tom" Warren, Wolverhampton, England, president of Rotary International, at a dinner meeting Monday night at 7 o'clock at the State street Methodist church.

An attendance of about 380 persons, including 12 past district governors, is expected to hear Mr. Warren's address, which will be the principal feature of the meeting.

Local men who formerly served District 161 as its governor are W. J. Craig, W. L. Matthews and J. Murray Hill. John Whitaker, of Russellville, is the present district governor and the Rev. Fred P. Turner is president of the Bowling Green Club. The Rev. Mr. Turner will preside.

A program feature to immediately precede President Warren's address will be a vocal solo by Joseph MacPherson, formerly a leading bass-baritone of the Metropolitan Opera Company. Mr. MacPherson is heralded by musical exponents as the outstanding singer of the south and is said to have taken his place among the best-known artists of the day. A favorite with Tennesseans the visiting artist has had six busy seasons with Metropolitan and has the wealth of experience lending maturity to his art and an all-time place with the masters.

The complete program will be as follows: invocation, Rotarian Bill Bolles; toastmaster's remarks, John Whitaker, district governor; solo, Mr. MacPherson; introduction of guests; solo, Mr. MacPherson, address, Mr. Warren.

The visiting speaker, in his own country has long been acknowledged as a speaker of national repute on educational and allied topics. His deepest interest is in the underpriviliged and ailing children, with whom he has dealt for many years. He, in addition to honors and attainments previously cited, was a member of the British Home Secretary's Advisory Committee for delinquent children and gave evidence before the commission, whose findings resulted in a Children's and Young Person's Act, which changed

(Continued on page 2, column 4)

Article dated 10-7-1945

Article dated 10-24-1945

Pays Tribute To Undersea Craft

(Continued on page 6, column 4)

"The full story of submarine sinkings of enemy vessels in the Pacific will never be told because of subs that did the work did not come back, but it is known that the undersea service destroyed more major enemy units than anything else," Petty Officer Arthur C. Erd, veteran of Pacific warfare disclosed at the Rotary club today.

Of the 318 major Japanese ships sunk by American forces more than one-third of the number were accounted for by submarine, the speaker who was brought to Bowling Green by the local Navy League Chapter declared. Many other problems were not counted because the U-Boat had to submerge before pictures showing the full extent of damage to the enemy could be taken, he pointed out.

The only thing the American Navy had left after Pearl Harbor was submarines, because the Japs failed to bomb sub bases in Hawaii and at Manila when surface units were nearly all disabled. He told how one Jap carrier was sunk in less than minutes after its launching by a daring Yank sub that laid wait for it in the enemy harbor. Carlson's Raiders were put ashore by intrepid subskippers for their telling raids on the enemy.

He asserted that enemy submarines were the most feared enemy of the American underwater craft but that in their encounters the Yank subs held a decided edge. Among his most harrowing experiences was an occasion when a bomb from an American B-24 struck his submarine but failed to explode.

The Navy Day speaker was introduced by Spl/c (R) Sanford Black who paid a glowing tribute to the work of the undersea service.

The club voted to accept its quota of $105,000 in the 8th Victory loan and Dr. J. L. Harman accepted the chairmanship of drive for the club. He announced that the same committees that functioned in the Mighty 7th War Loan would compose the organization for this campaign. Felix Allen, county chairmen, and J. Murray Hill, of the War Finance Committee spoke briefly pointing out that the Rotary club had throughout the seven previous war loans led the other civic clubs in obtaining their quotas.

The board of directors recommendation that a $100 gift be made to the Victory Fund and Community Chest was adopted, as was the boards recommendation for a $10 prize to the soil conservation contest for Warren county.

D. Rouglass Willock, the club's representative on a Red Cross Camp and Hospital Council tour to Fort Knox Monday, spoke briefly.

Guests were the Rev. G. W. Hummel, Madisonville, formerly of this city; Felix Allen, city; W. B. Pence, Jr., U. S. N., Allen Dodd, city; Rotarians M. C. Neal, Ray Scott, John Buck, and W. C. Howlett, all of Auburn; Pete Hancock, Russellville and George Donohue, Horse Cave.

L&N To Put New Streamliner In Operation

The Louisville and Nashville railroad plans to put into service this spring a new, streamlined train on its route between Cincinnati and New Orleans which passes through Bowling Green, Charles M. Cox, division freight agent for the road with offices in Nashville, told the noon meeting of the Rotary club today at the Helm hotel.

The L.&N. is expecting delivery this spring on 28 aluminum streamlined coaches with the latest modern facilities for travel, the speaker said. He stated that a new type of sleeping car and coaches for low rate day travel will be available to the public in the near future.

IMPROVING ROAD BEDS

Mr. Cox said that the railroad is improving its road beds, laying heavier rails and eliminating curves in preparation for safer operation of high speed trains.

Other new equipment has been ordered, he continued, including 2,000 new freight cars costing $7,700,000, eight new passenger engines totaling $1,400,000 and 19 additional diesel switch engines.

The speaker prefaced his remarks by saying that the L.&N. is Bowling Green's "oldest and largest single industry." He said that 150 employees of the company with a monthly payroll of $20,000 live here.

Mr. Cox asserted that the railroad in 1944 paid taxes in Bowling Green and Warren county totaling $45,806.71. Schools of the city and county received $19,976.71 of this amount, he added.

Guests were W. L. Matthews Jr., Frank H. Moore and George Williamson Jr., all of this city; Pete Hancock, Russellville; J. A. Barlow, New Albany, Ind.; Rotarians R. M. Armstrong and Albert Boyd, Franklin.

Elvis Campbell introduced Tandy —— ember. Paul Mar— agent.

Article dated 1-30-1946

Civic Groups Told World Should Share Our Heritage

7-28-48 Daily news

Although the Freedom Train is America's by heritage, what it symbolizes must be brought to all the people of the world, Ben Kilgore of Franklin told civic leaders at a luncheon at the Helm hotel Thursday.

"We have a rendezous with destiny, that of permitting other nations to share in our heritage," the assistant manager of the Eastern Dark Fired Tobacco Association told some 150 Rotarians, Kiwanians, Lions and guests at the Helm hotel.

Speaking at the official opening of "Rededication Week" ceremonies, which are preliminary to the visit of the Freedom Train here Monday, Mr. Kilgore envisioned the train as more than a machine bearing historical documents.

* * *

"IT IS A great revival," he said, "a revival to awaken our spirit, inspire us to a greater America, enable us to endure the hardships and fatigue which are the lot of those who would have liberty and permit others to share it."

Mr. Kilgore listed some of the documents on the train and pointed out how they symbolize the growth not alone of the United States but of the individuals who make up the country. He called for a true rededication to the principles evidenced in those documents so that "the mission of America to mankind may be accomplished."

Mr. Kilgore was introduced by J. David Francis, president of the local Junior Chamber of Commerce, sponsors of the train's visit here. J. Temp Flowers, president of the Kiwanis club, presided.

"REDEDICATION Week" ceremonies are to continue Friday when a special chapel program is scheduled at Van Meter hall on Western State college campus. Circuit Judge John B. Rodes is to be the principal speaker on the program, which opens at 10 a. m.

Saturday afternoon at 2:30 o'clock in Fountain Square Judge Rodes is to deliver another address in connection with the train's visit. The speech is to be broadcast over Daily News Radio Station WKCT.

E. O. Pearson Jr., chairman of the arrangement committee, is to officiate at the speaker's stand. Local Boy Scouts are to present the colors and lead in the pledge of allegiance.

A parade originally scheduled to precede the address has been cancelled, officials announced.

The train is to be on display at the L&N passenger station at 401 Kentucky street from 10 o'clock Monday morning until 10 o'clock that night. Admission is free.

Daily News article, dated 7-28-48

Article recounts a joint meeting among the Rotary, Kiwanis, and Lions Clubs

---

Max B. Nahm, Banker, Financier, Dies At 93

MAX B. NAHM

Max Brunswick Nahm, 93, millionaire financier and banker, died unexpectedly in his sleep early today at his home, 1403 College St. Funeral arrangements are incomplete. The body is at the Gerard - Bradley Chapel.

The elderly financier, one of the founders of the Citizens National Bank, was considered Southern Kentucky's wealthiest citizen. He was still active in business and was out yesterday. The banker served as a director of the Federal Reserve Bank of St. Louis for more than 40 years. Before becoming director of the St. Louis Bank, he was president of that bank's branch in Louisville.

At the time of his death, he was serving his 57th consecutive year as a director of the Citizens Bank here. He was also vice president of the institution. Nahm had also been a member of the board of directors of the Bowling Green Bank and Trust Company since its founding in 1911.

The banker gained state - wide recognition and was named Kentucky's "most useful citizen of 1929" for his efforts in the movement to establish Mammoth Cave as a national park.

Nahm was a charter member of the Mammoth Cave National Park Association that was organized here in 1924. He succeeded the late U. S. Senator M. M. Logan as president of the association and served in that capacity until the group's work was taken over by the Kentucky National Park Commission.

Nahm was then named chairman of the state commission. He served with the commission until the 1940's when he resigned.

* * *

Nahm first entered business here in 1887 as a member of the firm of E. Nahm and Company, operators of a men's clothing store.

From this start, he built a financial empire, remaining with the clothing firm until 1925.

Nahm was born here June 8, 1864, the only child of Emanuel Nahm and Rosa Brunswick Nahm. He graduated from Ogden College in 1883 and from Princeton University in 1885.

Nahm married Miss Sunshine Friedman of Paducah on Jan. 21, 1892. She died in 1937.

Nahm has served as president of the Ogden College Foundation which finances college scholarships for worthy Bowling Green and Warren County students.

For many years, he was leader in the work of the American Bankers Association, serving as the association's vice president from Kentucky in 1917.

Oth positions held with the national association included, member of the executive council, 1922-1925; chairman of federal legislative committee, 1924-25; member of the economic policy commission, 1926-1927 and 1931-1933; delegate to the International Chamber of Commerce, Amsterdam, Netherlands, 1929, and member of committee on revision of the National Banking Act in 1933.

He also served as president of the Kentucky Bankers Association in 1916.

* * *

Nahm was a director of the Federal Housing Administration for Kentucky in 1934-1935 and was appointed a member of the State Recovery Board of the National Recovery Administration in 1933. He actively served on numerous other governmental and civic commissions and organizations.

The financier was the last surviving charter member of the Bowling Green Elks Lodge and was a life member of the local Kiwanis Club.

Nahm was past president of the Lions Club and a past president of the Calendar Club, a literary group, and the Bowling Green Country Club. He also held membership in the Pendennis Club of Louisville and the Missouri Athletic Club.

He was a member of the Bowling Green City Council from 1901-1904 and served in the City Park Commission in 1926.

Nahm directed Liberty Loan drives during World War I in Southern Kentucky.

Surviving the banker is a daughter, Mrs. Emanie Nahm Arling, New York City authoress; a grandaughter, Mrs. Jane Ellen Sachs Hodes, Philadelphia, and three great grandchildren.

Mrs. Arling is scheduled to arrive here this afternoon to complete arrangements.

Continued on page 4, column 5

Park City Daily News article, dated 3-20-1958

Dr. J. M. Hill Dies In Bowling Green

Headed College Of Commerce For 15 Of Its Most Crucial Years

Courier-Journal South Kentucky Bureau

Bowling Green, Ky., Jan. 27.—J. Murray Hill, Sr., president of Bowling Green Business University and College of Commerce during 15 of its most crucial years, died Friday.

The 69-year-old educator had been hospitalized here since suffering a heart attack Sunday night.

Hill attended the business university and became its accountant and a member of its faculty in 1914. He was named an administrator in 1921 and served as a vice-president for 21 years before being named to succeed the late Dr. J. L. Harman as president in 1945.

'We Are Shocked'

Thus Hill presided over the school during its postwar growth and its being placed in the hands of a nonprofit corporation only last January 1.

Hill, vice-presidents W. L. Matthews, Sr., and J. Lewie Harmon, Jr., and long-time faculty member, William S. Fuqua, owned the school until turning it over to the corporation.

The new board named each to retain his post at the 800-student school. Chairman J. T. Orendorf said the board will not move hastily in naming a new president.

"We are shocked by the passing of Dr. Hill, and the loss of his leadership and inspiration will be a blow," Orendorf said.

Moved There In 1884

"But we feel we have highly competent leadership in vice-presidents Matthews and Harman so we have no plans to fill the presidency immediately."

The school, founded as the Glasgow Normal School at Glasgow in 1874, was moved here in 1884. Various name changes culminated by its being called the Bowling Green College of Commerce, formerly Bowling Green Business University under the nonprofit setup.

Hill, tall and quiet, but affable, was active in civic, business and educational circles.

He was a member of the boards of the College of Commerce, the Bowling Green Bank & Trust Company, and Citizens National Bank, where he was also a vice-president.

Served In Navy

He was a member of a number of education, civic, and social organizations, former president of the Southern Commercial Teachers Association, executive secretary of the Na-

J. MURRAY HILL, SR.

ciation, and director of the Mammoth Cave National Park Association.

Hill served in the Navy in World War I, was coauthor of a textbook on salesmanship, and was a past director and district governor of Rotary International. A wide traveler, he had spoken before Rotary clubs in Cairo, Jerusalem, and London.

Funeral Today

He is survived by his wife, Mrs. Ruth Elizabeth Phillips Hill; two daughters, Mrs. Frank H. Moore and Mrs. Harper Wright, both of Bowling Green; two sons, J. Murray Hill, Jr., Bowling Green, and Hoyt G. Hill, Nashville; three sisters, Mrs. Otis Fisher, Houston, Tex.; Mrs. Van C. Nall, Tyler, Tex., and Mrs. Hugh Jenkins, Glendale, and 13 grandchildren.

The funeral will be conducted by Dr. H. Franklin Paschall and the Rev. Fred Pfisterer at 2:30 p.m. Saturday at State Street Methodist Church. Burial will be in Fairview Cemetery here.

The body will remain at Gerard-Bradley Funeral Chapel until 12:30 p.m. Saturday. Then it will lie in state at the church until time for the funeral.

Hildreth Wins Rotary Club Golf Tourney

Carroll Hildreth captured the annual Rotary Club golf tournament at Bowling Green Country Club yesterday with a gross 77, six strokes over par.

Low net awards went to J. H. Webb, Roland Fitch and B. C. Parker, all of whom had 71s.

Nineteen members of the club competed in the event.

Article dated 6-21-1961

Courier-Journal article dated 1-28-61

Governor To Speak At Joint Meeting Of Rotary Clubs

Gov. Bert Combs will address a joint meeting of the Bowling Green and Auburn Rotary clubs at 12 noon Wednesday during his visit to Bowling Green. The meeting is set for Olde Fort restaurant.

The governor is scheduled to arrive Wednesday morning and backed up by a 14-member staff will conduct state business from his temporary headquarters at the State Highway Department district office building on Morgantown Road.

He also will speak Wednesday morning at Western State College and will be special guest at Chamber of Commerce luncheon at noon Thursday prior to leaving

Article dated 7-24-1961

ALONZO MOREHEAD CAUSEY
Rotarian Nearing 100

Articles dated 1970

H. W. Sublett Was There

Harold Watson Sublett was born March 26, 1880, on a farm located about eight miles out on the Morgantown Road, and is the son of the late Samuel Benson Sublett and the late Lura Dean Wiley Sublett.

Sublett moved to Bowling Green with his parents in 1888 and started work in a drug store owned by George Wilson. This store was located on the corner of State Street and Park Row where Woolworth's now is. The firm of Carpenter-Dent-Sublett was formed in 1912 with T??his Carpenter and Carpenter's son-in-law, Emory Dent.

Sublett served as treasurer of Warren County in 1915 and was on the city council under Mayor John B. Rodes from 1929 until 1933. Sublett was appointed postmaster here in 1940 and occupied that position until 1949.

Sublett is a charter member of the Bowling Green Rotary Club, having joined in 1920. He is the only living charter member and was also the first treasurer of the Rotary Club. He has always taken an interest in Rotary and attended the International Rotary Convention held in Los Angeles in 1922.

He is the oldest member of both the I.O.O.F. and B.P.O.E. and though he is not the oldest member of State Street United Methodist Church, he has been a member longer than anyone else.

Sublett was married to Miss Bettie Buckner in 1907 and Mrs. Sublett died in 1960. His children are Miss Sara Dean Sublett, with whom he resides at 1714 Nashville Road, and Robert Sublett, of Louisville.

Though 90 now, Sublett looks forward to the Rotary Club meetings and still attends regularly every Wednesday.

ROTARY WORLDWIDE
Each week, Rotary meetings are called to order in dozens of different languages.

But regardless of how they say it, Rotarians in 148 countries go about their task with one objective in mind: the improvement of their city, state or province and nation.

HAROLD W. SUBLETT

Prior to 1973 when the Belle burned

Photo dated 1985

David Garvin invited the club to meet at his new horse barn in 1994. We had charcoal grilled hamburgers and the works.

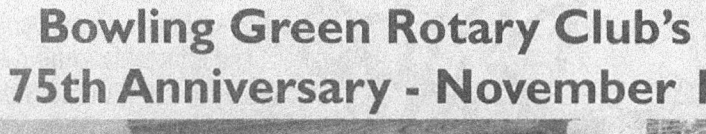

The Bowling Green Rotary Club will celebrate its 75th anniversary on November 1, 1995, with a dinner at the Bowling Green Country Club. Mayor Johnny Webb and County Judge Executive Mike Buchanan (seated) have just signed a Joint Proclamation fixing Wednesday, November 1 as Rotary Day in Bowling Green and Warren County. Looking on from left to right (standing) are Vickie Elrod, Larry Pack, Robbie Bond, Mark Hildreth, Bob Schulten, Gary Dillard, Ken Mullins, Bob Kleier, Jerry Parker, Rick DuBose, President Chuck Coates and Secretary Bob Long.

Format of Weekly Meetings

The format for the weekly Rotary meetings of our Club is the following and this for the most part has always been the format for all Rotary Clubs, maybe with a few variations:

    Lunch
    Prayer
    Pledge
    Introduction of Guests
    Program
*Selection of Mr. "R"
    Recitation (in Unison) of the Four Way Test

* The Mr. "R" convention encourages members to greet each other (hand shake) and small talk. One member (in advance) is designated to select Mr./Mrs. "R". The fifth person to shake the designees' hand is the Mr. "R" for that week.

The Four Way Test- of the things we think, say or do:
1.) Is it the truth?
2.) Is it fair to all concerned?
3.) Will it build good will and better friendships?
4.) Will it be beneficial to all concerned?

The Presidents

1920-2009

| Whit Potter | J.O. Carson | A.S. Hines | J.E. Tyler |
| 1920-1922 | 1922-1923 | 1923-1924 | 1924-1925 |

photo not available

| H.H. Cherry | Frank Cole | Garland Sledge | Lawrence B. Finn |
| 1925-1926 | 1926-1927 | 1927-1928 | 1928-1929 |

| P.C. Deemer | Sam Cristal | James M. Hill | A.J. Miller |
| 1929-1930 | 1930-1931 | 1931-1932 | 1932-1933 |

| W.L. Matthews | W.C. Sumpter | L.T. Smith | J.R. Meany |
| 1933-1934 | 1934-1935 | 1935-1936 | 1936-1937 |

| George H. Moseley | R. Douglas Willock | J.T. (Top) Orendorf | J. Murray Hill, Sr. |
| 1937-1938 | 1938-1939 | 1939-1940 | 1940-1941 |

Paul L.
Garrett
1941-1942

Hubert
Cherry
1942-1943

J.H. (Jake)
Bernard
1943-1944

J.C. Holland
1944-1945

Fred Turner
1945-1946

Maurice Hill
1946-1947

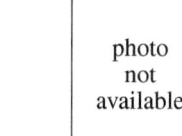
Basil Pence
1947-1948

W.O. Dotson,
Jr.
1948-1949

Fred Spires
1949-1950

J.D. Monin,
Jr.
1950-1951

Ward C.
Sumpter
1951-1952

R.E. Gaddie
1952-1953

C.B. Talbert
1953-1954

Roland Fitch,
Jr.
1954-1955

Herbert
Smith, Sr.
1955-1956

Charles H.
Hildreth
1956-1957

Wendell
Groves
1957-1958

Elvis
Campbell
1958-1959

John Milliken
1959-1960

Walter
Nalbach
1960-1961

W. Kenton
Mullins
1961-1962

Charles R.
Bryant
1962-1963

L.O. Toomey
1963-1964

Joseph E.
Davenport
1964-1965

Skiles Harris
1965-1966

Lewis
Graham
1966-1967

Lee C.
Truman
1967-1968

Carroll
Hildreth
1968-1969

William J.
(Jerry) Parker
1969-1970

Grover
Holderfield
1970-1971

Henry
Carlisle, Jr.
1971-1972

Mark Easton,
III
1972-1973

John
Scarborough
1973-1974

Henry Pepper
1974-1975

David Cole
1975-1976

C.H. (Tuffey)
Jeannette
1976-1977

Harold
Brantley
1977-1978

Tom Hall
1978-1979

Charles M.
Moore, Jr.
1979-1980

Charles
Hardcastle
1980-1981

Spero G.
Kereiakes
1981-1982

Kenneth R.
Wallace
1982-1983

Joe Cook
1983-1984

Joel Rogers
1984-1985

Mike Hepp
1985-1986

Randy Capps
1986-1987

Tommy
Holderfield
1987-1988

James E.
Johnson
1988-1989

Wade
Markham
1989-1990

David
Buchanan
1990-1991

Wayne Priest
1991-1992

Craig Evans
1992-1993

Ron
Shrewsbury
1993-1994

Rick Dubose
1994-1995

Charles
W. Coates
1995-1996

Robert
Soncrant
1996-1997

Gary K.
Dillard
1997-1998

Deborah G.
Catron
1998-1999

Larry J. Pack
1999-2000

Ben Smith
2000-2001

193 | Presidents

John Minton
2001-2002

Mark
Hilldreth
2002-2003

Steve Wilson
2003-2004

Jerald W.
Manning
2004-2005

Vicki Elrod
2005-2006

Shannon
Morgan
2006-2007

Alex
Downing
2007-2008

Mac
Jefferson
2008-2009

Kevin Mays
2009-2010

Gallery

1955 Roster

Henry H. Baird

J.H. Barnard

Marvin E. Brown

Phillip E. Binzel

James W. Brite

James David Bryant

Joseph E. Davenport

Paul C. Deemer

Paul C. Deemer, Jr.

Leonard Raymond Deloteus

Hubert Cherry

Charles H. Clark

Otis Vernon Clark Jr.

G. Frank Cole

Samuel Coombs Cooke

Joe S. Dickson

Allen Leroy
Dodd, Sr.

W. Kenton
Mullins

John D.
Faulkner

Roland Fitch,
Jr.

Dr. Charles
M. Francis

Eli B.
Friedman

Joseph F.
Fuqua

Guy Fuson

Roy E.
Gaddie

John B.
Gaines

J. Ray Gaines

Joe F. Garnett

Guthrie
Yoehlee
Graves, M.D.

Dr. Hollis
Allen Gray

Jas. R. Hines

J. Cecil
Holland

V. "Ted"
Hornback

Ervin G.
Houchens

W. Wilson
Hourigan

Wendell H.
Groves

J. Lewie
Harman, Sr.

J. Lewie
Harman, Jr.

Paul M.
Harrison

Charles H.
Hildreth

Phares
Alexander
Hughes

J. Tilden
Orendorf

Aubrey
Johnson

L.O. Johnson

C.W.
Lampkin

James M. Hill

Maurice A.
Hill

Alonzo M.
Causey

Murray Hill,
Jr.

Duncan L.
Hines

Martin S.
Leventhal

Mitchell
Leichhardt

Joseph H.
McFarland

Wallace
McGinley

John C.
McKissick

B.C. Parker

J. Russell
Meany

Frank G.
Melton

Judge John
M. Milliken

A.J. Miller

James D.
Monin, Jr.

Frank H.
Moore, M.D.

Frank P.
Moore

J. William
(Bill) Moore

George H.
Mosley

Roy C.
Phillips

Robert W.
Moulder

W.E. Ray

Garland
Reeves

William L.
Roemer

Henry L.
Stephens

Charles M.
Stewart

Harold
Watson
Sublett

Col. William
Cullin
Sumpter

Ward C.
Sumpter

Gordon Smith

| Hebert J. Smith | L.T. Smith | David L. Sneed | Fred Spires |

| Clifford B. Talbert | James R. Thompson | Dr. L.O. Toomey | Oscar Uhl |

| J.H. Webb | Robert Douglas Willock | Theo Withers | Elvis Richard Campbell |

1970 Roster

| B.H. Adams | Leslie Allen | Henry Baird | Thomas H. Baird |

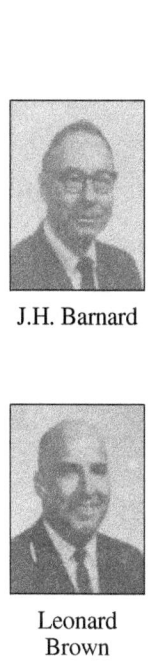 J.H. Barnard

 H.H. Barney

 J.R. Bettersworth, Jr.

 James Brite

 Leonard Brown

Marvin Brown

 William Brown

 Charles Bryant

 Robert Bueker

 Elvis R. Campbell

 Randall Capps

 Henry Carlisle, Jr.

 Geo. E. Carpenter

 A. M. Causey

 J. Joe Cheek

 Hubert Cherry

 O.V. Clark, Jr.

 G. Frank Cole

 David Cole

 Jerry W. Conder

 S.C. Cooke
 Keith Coverdale
 Crawford Crowe
 Joe Davenport

 Edward DiBella
 A.L. Dodd
 Kelsey Driskell
 Mark Eastin

 Jody Ellis
 Bob Eudy
 John B. Faulkner
 Ron Ferguson

 Roland Fitch
 Lucas Floyd,, Jr.
 Joe T. Fuqua
 R.E. Gaddie

 Joe F. Garnett
 Ronald Garvin
 J.T. Graham
 Lewis Graham

| Hollis Gray | Lewis Graybeal | Tom Hall | Charles Hardcastle |

| Skiles Harris | Leo Hartman | John Herrick | Claude Herrin |

| Charles Heyduck | Ted Hightower | Carroll Hildreth | Charles Hildreth |

| James M. Hill | Maurice Hill | James R. Hines | Wellington Hines |

| Grover Holderfield | J.C. Holland | V.T. Hornback | Ervin Houchens |

William
Hourigan

Robert
Hovious

Paul
Hudspeth

Tommy
Hughes

Richard
Jackel

Howard
Jeannette

Aubrey
Johnson

Norris Jolly

N.Z. Kafoglis

Thomas L.
Kelley, Jr.

Ralph King

Gary
Kissenger

R.B. Kramer

Dick
Lacefield

Mitchell
Leichhardt

Robert Long

J.H.
McFarland

Henry N.
Meiers

A.J. Miller

John Milliken

 Tom Montgomery

 J. William Moore

 Robert Moulder

 Ray Mullendore

 W.K. Mullins

 Walter Nalbach

 Douglas T. Norton

 Tom Nuckols

 Jo T. Orendorf

 Henry Padgett

 William J. Parker

 Henry Pepper

 R.C. Phillips

 Garland Reeves

 Charles Reynolds

 Nelson Rue

 Clem Russell

 Marvin Russell

 John Scarbrough

 Frank Six

Charles B. Smith Gilbert Smith Herbert Smith L.T. Smith

Fred Spires Harold Stahl H.L. Stephens Charles Stewart

Wes Strader Harold Sublett Ward Sumpter Howard Surface

Richard Thalacker Lee Truman L.O. Toomey Thomas Updike

Al Vaughn Marcus Wallace J.H. Webb Joe P. Wilk

Perry
Williams

Jim
Willoughby

Sterling
Willoughby

Harold Wills

William E.
Wortham

1978 Roster

Dr. S. Basheer
Ahmed

Thomas H.
Baird

E. Wallace
Barr, Jr.

Henry H.
Baird

Dr. John
Blackburn

Marvin
Brown

Bill Brown

Charles R.
Bryant

207 | Gallery

James David Bryant

Robert Bueker

Rev. Rollin Burhans

Randy Capps

Henry Carlisle

Steve Carver

J. Joe Cheek

O.V. Clark, Jr.

Frank G. Cole

John David Cole

Joseph E. Davenport

John C. Desmarais

Edward Engel DiBella

Brents Dickinson III

Jack Dillard

Kelcy Driskill

Joseph J. Duffy

Mark E. Eastin III

Bob M. Eudy

Harold Evans

 Baun Everley

 Gene C. Farley

 John D. Faulkner

 Earl Fisher

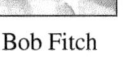 Bob Fitch

 Harry Ford

 Pipes Gaines

 Earnest Garner

 Joseph F. Garnett

 David Garvin

 Wendell Gentry

 Claude Gibson

 Greg Gibson

 A.F. Godby

 J.T. Graham

 Lewis W. Graham

 Dr. Hollis A. Gray

 Jimmie Greenway

 I. Thomas Grogan

 Robert L. Hancock

209 | Gallery

Riley Handy

Charles Hardcastle

Skiles Harris

Leo J. Hartman

Robert N. Henon

John S. Herrick

C. Carroll Hildreth

Jim Hill

Maurice A. Hill

Jimmy Hines

Wellington Hines

Grover C. Holderfield

Tommy Holderfield

Ted Hornback

Ervin Houchens

W.R. Hourigan

Bob Hovious

Danny A. Howell

Tommy Hughes

Joe D. Hunt

 R. Harvey Johnston III
 Norris Jolly
 W. Basil Jones, Jr.
 Thomas L. Kelley, Jr.

 Robert B. Krammer
 Richard S. Lacefield, Jr.
 Richard S. Lacefield, Sr.
 Robert F. Lancaster

 Mitchell Leichhardt
 Barry V. Locke
 Robert C. Long
 Caroll M. Luckey

 Lee Martin
 Joseph Hardin McFarland, Sr.
 Joseph Hardin McFarland, Jr.
 Grant McKibben

 Kenneth A. Meredith, Sr.
 Kenneth A. Meredith II
 A.J. Miller
 John Milliken

Charles M. Moore, Jr.

J. William Moore

Robert Moulder

Howard Ray Mullendore

William Kenton Mullins

Walter B. Nelbach

Gordon Boyd Newell

William Randall Odil

Charles Louis Owsley

William Jerry Parker

James A. Parrish, Jr.

Henry Pepper

John C. Perkins

George E. Peterson, Jr.

Lee Pope

David E. Rabold

Garland Reeves

John W. Ridley

Norbert A. Rubano

Nelson B. Rue, Jr.

Clem W. Russell	John Scarborough	Jim Shanahan	Charles B. Smith

Gilbert H. Smith	Herb Smith	Stephen Page Smith	Charles Stewart

Rev. H. Howard Surface, Jr.	Fred L. Tanner	John Tapscott	L.O. Toomey

Lee Truman	Thomas L. Updike, Jr.	M.A. Vaughn	Donald P. Wendt

Joseph P. Wilk	Perry T. Williams	Roland D. Willock	James O. Willoughby

 Sterling Willoughby

 Harold Wills

 Charles Ray Woosley

 William E. Wortham

 Thomas L. Yelton

1995 Roster

 Buddy Adams

 Jim Adams

 Gary Asbury

 Joe Baden

 Tom Baird

 Mike Binder

 Mike Bishop

 John Blackburn

| Dale Bond | Bill Brantley | Charlie Brumit | Charles Bryant |

| Mike Buchanon | Bob Bueker | John Burks | Paul Cannon |

| John Carmon | Keith Carwell | Lloyd Cassady | Debbie Catron |

| Joe Cheek | Dan Cherry | H.B. Clark, Jr. | Chuck Coates |

| Murray Coker | David Cole | Keith Coverdale | Gil Crouch |

215 | Gallery

Bart Hagerman

Charles Hardcastle

Bob Haynes

Carrol Hildreth

Tommy Holderfield

Bill Hourigan

Dan Howell

Joe Huddleston

Philip Huddleston

Tom Hughes

Joe Hunt

Tim Huston

Jack Jacobsen

Rolla Jefferson

Jim Johnson

Fred Keith

Kevin Kirby

Gary Larimore

Mark Linder

Bob Long

 Howard Surface

 Joe Taylor

 Tony Torres

 Lee Truman

 LeRoy Underwood

 Mike Voyles

 Tony Walker

 Ken Wallace

 Ed Weldon

 Don Wendt

 Mark Woodward

 Dan McIvor

 Jim Weisz

 Bill Dewhurst

 Phillip Lance

 Bill Jacobson

 Dana Carrier

2009 Roster

James R. Adams

Patricia Alford

Cheryl Allen

Jim Allen

Steve Ayers

Shaun Ayres

Thomas Baird H., M.D.

Michael J. Barron

Dr. Richard Beaven

James Bennett

John Blackburn, M.D.

Janette Boehman

Johnston Boyd

Harold Brantley

Mike Buchanon

Robert Bueker

221 | Gallery

Paul Edward Cannon

Mary Ann Carmon

Linda Chambers

Dan Cherry

H.B. Clark, Jr.

Chris Cohron

Ward Coleman

Thad Connally, III

Kevin Counts

Matthew Covington

E. Margaret Curtis

Joe Davis

John Deeb

Barbara DeFebbo

Brents Dickinson, III

Alex Downing

Rick DuBose

Floyd Ellis

Vickie Elrod

Ken Embry

Gene Farley

Chris Graham

Dr. Lewis W. Graham

John Grider

John Grise

Brian Gugler

Jack Hanes

Charlie Hardcastle

Donna Harmon

Walter Aden Hawkins

Bill Helmbold

Carrol C. Hildreth

Mark Hildreth

Kenneth B. Hines, Sr.

Nathan Hodges

Catherine Rice Holderfield

Tommy Holderfield

Robert Hovious

Danny Howell

Joseph Huddleston

Joe Hunt

Jack Jacobsen

Mac Jefferson

W. Basil Jones

Travis Keller

Jeff Keyes

Cheryl Kirby-Stokes

Bob Kleier

Joe Liles

Cliff Long

Robert Long

Scott Lowe

Michael D. Manship

Kevin Mays

Kent McBrayer

Joseph McFarland

William McKenzie

Richard Miller

Amy Milliken

John Minton Jr.

 Charles Moore
 Shannon Morgan
 Paul Mysinger
 Larry Pack

 Alan Palmer
 Rachelle Phillips Shults
 Gary Pierce
 Robert Porter

 Whayne Priest, Jr.
 Sally Ray
 Mike Reynolds
 Jody Richards

 Hugh David Roe
 Alice Simpson
 Kevin Simpson
 Jim Skaggs

 Ben Smith
 Charles "Chuck" Smith
 Charles W. Smith
 Janet Bass Smith

Ryan Smith

Col. Robert Spiller

Rev. Howard Surface

Joe W. Taylor

Jack A. Thomas

Linda Thomas

Lee Truman

LeRoy Underwood

Thomas L. Updike, Jr.

Alan Vilines

Kenneth Russell Webb

Bruce Wilkerson

Rick Williams

Ron Wilson

Steve Wilson

Mark Woodward, D.C.

Index of Members

Buddy Adams — 1969
Jim Adams — 1976
Robert Adams — 1991
Jacqueline Addington — 1995
Col. Richard Agnew
Dr. S. Basheer Ahmed — 1976
Frank Alden
Bob Aldridge — 1986
Patricia Alford — 1996
Cheryl Allen — 1998
Jim Allen — 1976
Leslie Allen — 1969
Sam Allen — 1920's
W. C. Almstedt — 1920's
Gary Asbury — 1993
Kevin Atwood — 1996
Shaun Ayers — 2006
Rev. Steve Ayers — 1995
Shaun Bachert
Scott Bachert – 2007
Joe Baden – 1991
Henry H. Baird — 1937
Dr. Thomas Baird — 1963
Hilliard Baker
Kirk Ballard — 1996
Joe H. Banet
James H. Barclay — 1920's
Jake Barnard — 1939
H. H. Barney — 1968
Dr. E. Wallace Barr — 1920's
E. Wallace Barr, Jr. (Sonny) — 1975
Bruce Barrick — 1980
Mike Barron — 2009
Dr. Craig Beard — 1988
Dr. Mike Beaven — 2002
Arch Bennett
James K. (Jim) Bennett — 2003
J.R. Bettersworth — 1963
H.D. Biggs
Mike Binder — 1993
Phillip E. Binzel — 1936
Mike Bishop — 1994
Dr. John Blackburn — 1971
Janette Boehman — 2006
James Bohannon — 1930's

Carey Boles
Douglas Bolling — 1920's
Dale Bond — 1992
Henry Bradley — 1920's
Tim Bradshaw — 1996
Bill Brantley — 1992
Harold Brantley —1970
James W. Brite — 1955
Kevin Brooks — 1996
Willliam H. Brown — 1969
Marvin E. Brown — 1942
Will Allen Brown
Leonard D. Brown — 1968
William Brown
Harold Brown — 1968
J. Michael Brown — 1992
Charlie Brummit — 1990
Phillip Brunson — 1940's
James David Bryant — 1954
Charles R. Bryant — 1949
David Bryant, Jr. — 1994
Michael Buchanan —2005
Bob Bueker —1968
Dr. Frank Buono
Holly Burch — 1920's
Rev. Rollin Burhans — 1974
John Burks — 1985
Guy Byrn — 1920's
Martin Caldwell
Gilbert Calhoun — 2005
Travis Calvert — 2006
Elvis Richard Campbell — 1943
Paul Canon — 1992
Randy Capps— 1969
Thomas Cargill
Henry Carlisle — 1965
Alisa Carmichael — 2004
Mary Carmon
John Carmon — 1998
George Carpenter — 1970
Dana Carrier — 1993
Dr. J. O. Carson — 1920 (charter)
Dr. Fred D. Cartwright — 1920 (charter)
Steve Carver — 1972
Keith Carwell — 1980

Lloyd W. Cassady — 1989
Dr. Deborah Catron — 1991
Mike Caudill — 1978
Alonzo (Lon) M. Causey — 1928
Linda Chambers — 2003
Rev. George W. Cheek — 1926
Dr. J. Joe Cheek — 1960
Morton Chelf
Hubert Cherry — 1938
Dr. H.H. Cherry — 1922
Gen. Dan Cherry — 1989
Charles H. Clark — 1948
Otis V. Clark, Jr. — 1948
H. B. Clark, Jr. — 1990
Otis V. Clark, Sr. — 1930's
George Claypool — 1920's
Phillip Clendenin
Col. Gordon Coates
Charles D. (Chuck) Coates — 1982
Christopher Cohron — 2003
Mary Cohron — 2006
Murray Coker — 1979
G. Frank Cole — 1951
Rev. A.E. Cole
Frank W. Cole
Frank G. Cole — 1951
John David Cole 1968
John David Cole, Jr. —1996
Ward Coleman — 1999
Jerry W. Conder — 1970
Thad Connally, III — 2005
Samuel Coombs Cook — 1924
Joseph A. Cook II — 1971
Kevin Counts — 2004
Dr. Courtney Olney – 1998
Dr. Keith Coverdale — 1967
Rev. Matthew Covington — 2002
W. J. Craig — 1920 (charter)
Tim Creasy — 1990's
D. S. Crisp
Samuel Cristal — 1920 (charter)
Gil Crouch — 1984
Carol Crowe-Carraco — 2006
Margaret Curtis — 1996
Sterett Cuthbertson — 1920 (charter)

Warth Dafal
Joseph H. Davenport — 1952
Joe Davis — 2000
John Deeb — 1986
Paul C. Deemer, Jr. — 1945
Paul C. (Pete) Deemer, Sr. — 1924
R. C. Deen
Barbara DeFebbo — 2007
Leonard Raymond Deloteus — 1950
Emory G. Dent — 1921
John C. Desmaris
Dr. Bill Dewhurst — 1994
Ed Di Bella — 1954
Brents Dickinson 1975
Joe S. Dickson — 1953
Gary Dillard— 1982
Jack Dillard
Allen Leroy Dodd, Jr. — 1953
Allen Leroy Dodd, Sr. — 1943
Steger Dollar
Dr. A. D. Donnelly
Troy C. Dossett — 1992
Wick Dotson
Kimberly Dowell— 2000
Alex Downing — 1998
William Draper
Kelly Driskill 1952
Rick Dubose — 1997
Joseph J. Duffy - 1976
Robert H. Dunnagan — 1994
Jeffrey Durham
Mark E. Easton, III — 1968
John Edwards
Rev. William Eisenhart — 1920's
Floyd Hays Ellis — 2000
Marty Elmes — 1996
Vickie Elrod — 1991
Dr. Ken Embry — 2003
Frank Ennis —1921
Noel (Sonny) Ennis — 1980
Bob Eudy — 1964
C. P. Evans — 1920 (charter)
Craig Evans — 1980
Harold Evans — 1976
Baun Everly — 1968

229 | Index of Members

Gene Farley — 1962
Ban Farnsworth — 1920's
John D. Faulkner — 1955
Trent Fergerson — 1992
Lawrence B. Finn — 1930's
Earl Fisher — 1974
Henry Fitch — 1920's
Robert R. Fitch — 1971
Roland Fitch, Jr. — 1938
Lucas Floyd, Jr. —1954
Alvin Ford — 2005
Harry Ford
M. C. Ford — 1930's
Dr. Charles M. Francis
J. David Francis — 1991
Eli B. Friedman — 1936
Henry W. Funk — 1921
Joseph F. Fuqua — 1936
Mike Fuqua — 1995
Guy Fuson
Roy E. Gaddie — 1948
John B. Gaines — 1940
Clarence M. Gaines
Pipes Gaines — 1977
J. Ray Gaines
Henry T. Galloway
Rex Galloway — 1986
Rev. Wedge E. Gamble
Ernest Garner — 1972
Joseph F. Garnett — 1945
Dr. Paul L. Garrett
Samuel Garvin
David Garvin — 1974
Ronald M. Garvin — 1969
Wendell Gentry — 1973
Don Gerard, Jr. — 2007
Dr. Abdol Ghayoumi — 2003
Claude Gibson — 1975
Greg Gibson — 1974
Dr. J. T. Gilbert
John Gillespie — 1995
Dr. Fogle Godby — 1970
Russ Goldberg — 1996
Frank Gonce
L.T. Goodride

Dr. Robert A. Goodwin
Douglas Gott — 1994
Amos Gott — 1995
Dave Gottfried — 1996
Lewis Grabill — 1968
Cris Graham — 2006
Dr. Lewis Graham — 1961
J.T. Graham
Lucian D. Graham, Jr.
Lucian D. Graham, Sr. — 1920's
W.B. Grant
Dr. G. Y. Graves — 1933
Dr. Coleman Graves
Dr. Hollis Gray — 1943
Jimmie Greenway — 1977
Edgar A. Greer
Shelby Greer
John Grider — 2002
John Grise — 2004
Tom Grogan — 1977
Wendell H. Groves — 1939
Ed Groves — 1996
Brian Gugler — 2008
Bart Hagerman — 1971
Dr. Tom Hall — 1969
Sam Hall — 1979
David Hancock — 1980
Robert L. Hancock — 1976
Riley Handy — 1976
Jack Hanes — 2006
Charles Hardcastle — 1969
Donna Harmon — 1998
J. Lewie Harman, Jr. — 1946
Dr. J. Lewie Harman, Sr. — 1922
Ennis D. Harris —1920's
Skiles Harris — 1959
Paul Harrison — 1953
Leo J. Hartman — 1962
Lowell Hatfield
Walter Hawkins — 1998
Bob Haynes — 1984
George E Heiner
Craig Heller — 1989
Dr. T. O.Helm — 1923
Bill Helmbold — 2007

Robert Henon — 1971
Dewey Henry
Mike Hepp — 1978
Guy H. Herdman — 1920's
John S. Herrick — 1967
Claude Herrin — 1957
C. Heyduck — 1968
Ray Hicks 2006
Heather Higgins — 2009
Rev. Ted Hightower — 1969
Charles H. Hildreth — 1938
Mark Hildreth — 1995
James M. Hill — 1928
Maurice Hill — 1939
William B. Hill — prior to 1955
J. Murray Hill, Jr. — 1947
J. Murray Hill, Sr. — 1921
Tom Hills — 1999
Scott H. Hines
A.Scott Hines — 1920 (charter)
Kenneth Hines — 2002
Wellington Hines — 1966
James R. Hines — 1950
Duncan L. Hines —1949
Warner W. Hines — 1920's
James R. Hoagland —Prior to 1955
Walker J. Hoagland
Dr. Nathan Hodges — 2005
Catherine Holderfield — 1992
Grover Holderfield — 1965
Tommy Holderfield — 1977
J.C. Holland — 1940
W.W. Holman — 1930's
Herbert A. Holstein — 1921
Ray Hopper — 1930's
V. Ted Hornback — 1947
Rev. John Burns Horton
Ervin G. Houchens — 1937
W. Wilson Hourigan — 1954
Ed Houston — 1994
Martin Houston — 1994
Ed Houston — 1994
Bob Hovious — 1966
Brad Howard — 2005
Sammy Howell — 1971

Danny Howell — 1971
Joe Huddleston — 1993
Margaret Huddleston — 2001
Phillip Huddleston — 1988
Paul R. Hudspeth — 1968
Phares Alexander Hughes — 1954
Tommy Hughes —1967
Dr. George W. Hummel — Prior to 1955
Joe Hunt — 1970
Ed Hurley —1992
Tim Huston — 1984
Carlton Hyde
Mark Iverson — 1993
Richard Jackel — 1964
Jack Jacobson — 1985
William W. (Bill) Jacobson, Sr. — 1990
Joseph C. Janes
Howard (Tuffy) Jeanette — 1969
Bob Jeffers —1993
Mac Jefferson — 1998
Rolla Jefferson — 1980
Bob Jefferson — 1996
James S. Johnson — 1980
Aubrey Johnson — 1955
Dr. L. O. Johnson — 1932
Andrew Johnson
Mark Johnson— 1995
Harvey Johnston — 1977
Norris Jolly — 1968
Buford E. Jones — 1930's
Basil Jones — 1976
Gary Jones — 1999
Guy S. Jones — 1920 (charter)
L.V. Steve Justice — 1991
Dr. Nick Kafoglis — 1967
Robert Kalm — 1920's
Fred Keith — 1978
Buddy Keith
Travis Keller — 2005
Tom Kelley — 1964
Tommy Kelley — 1997
Dr. Spero Kereiakes — 1972
Jeff Keyes — 2007
Lana Martin Kilgore — 1996
H.P. Kincaid

Ralph L. King — 1970
Maurice Kirby
Kevin Kirby — 1990
Gary Kissinger — 1970
Bob Kleier — 1972
Tom Koen
R.B. Kramer — 1942
Dr. Walter Kuebler —1993
Richard Lacefield, Jr. — 1971
Dick Lacefield, Sr. — 1956
C. W. Lampkin —1926
Robert F. Lancaster
Phillip Lance — 1994
Brad Lawrence
Mitchell Leichardt —1946
Martin S. Leventhal — 1945
Joe Liles — 2005
Rev. Mark Linder —1994
Barry V. Locke — 1967
Bob Long — 1960
Cliff Long — 1993
Dennis Longest — 2003
Marshall Love, Sr. — 1920's
Andy Lovell — 1986
Marc Lovell — 1993
Scott Lowe — 1984
Thaddeus Lucas — 2006
Carroll M. Luckey — 1976
R.L. Lusk
Mark Mackey — 2005
Charles T. Malling
Jane Manning —1996
Jerald Manning —1999
Charlie Manning —1930
Mike Manship —1997
Wade Markham — 1983
John Martin — 1930's
Paul E. Martin
J.C. Martin
Larry Martin —1994
Dr. Lee Martin
Bill Mason — 1986
George T. Massey —1920's
Russell Masters
S.M. Matlock — 1920's

W.L. Matthews — 1922
Kevin Mays — 2003
Kent McBrayer —1993
Joe McFarland, Jr. — 1976
Joseph (Joe) McFarland, Sr. — 1946
Wallace McGinley — 1946
Thomas McGown
Daniel McIvor —1992
Bill McKenzie — 1987
Grant McKibbin — 1977
Dr. John C. McKissick — 1946
James R. Meany — 1938
Dr. Henry Meiers — 1964
Frank G. Melton — 1934
Ken A. Meredith, II — 1977
Ken A. Meredith, Sr. — 1973
Cornell Meuking — 2008
Edward Mickel
A.J. Miller —1923
Richard Miller — 1990
John M. Milliken — 1953
Amy Milliken — 2005
Currie W. Milliken — 1971
John D. Minton, Jr. — 1992
James D. Monin, Jr. — 1946
Tom Montgomery — 1964
Ann Moore — 1994
Dr. Frank H. Moore —1949
Frank P. Moore —1923
J. William (Bill) Moore —1954
Hamp Moore —1979
William T. Moore — 2002
Dr. Bill T. Moore — 1993
Charles M. Moore, Jr. — 1970
Shannon Morgan — 1999
Robert Morris — 1920's
George H. Moseley — 1921
McElroy Moss
Robert W. Moulder — 1945
Howard Ray Mullendore — 1967
W. Kenton Mullins — 1954
Rev. Walter I Munday — 1923
Judy Myers — 1996
Paul Mysinger — 2006
Paul L. Nadeau —1995

Walter Nalbach — 1957
Dr. Baxter W. Napier
E. W. Neate
Dr. Gordan B. Newell — 1975
Alex Nottmeier — 2000
Dr. Tom Nuckols —1968
Col. Ray Nutter — 1985
Regis O'Connor — 1972
Wm. Randall Odil — 1977
Frank Odum
Dr. Courtney Olney, Sr. — 1998
J. Tilden Orendorf — 1935
Robert Osteen — 1920's
F.B. Ostermueller
Richard Owen
Dr. Charles L. Owsley
Julian Pace
Dr. Larry J. Pack — 1987
Henry Padgett — 1970
Yandell Page — 1920's
Alan Palmer — 1985
Roger M. Parish — 1930's
Gene Parker
B.C. Parker —1938
William J. (Jerry) Parker — 1959
James A. Parrish, Jr. — 1975
Tom Pearce —1983
A.W. Peete — 1921
Basil Pence -
Henry Pepper — 1969
Harris Pepper — 1992
Mit D. Perkins
John Perkins — 1977
George E. Peterson, Jr. — 1976
Roy T. Phillips — 1931
Rachelle Phillips — 2008
Roy C. Phillips, Jr. — 1949
Nixon Pichard
Gary Pierce — 2005
Lee Pope —1977
Robert (Rob) Porter — 1999
Paul Porter — 1973
J. Whit Potter — 1920 (charter)
Brent Potter — 2000
Sam Potter, Jr. — 1998

Dr. Paul Shell Powell — 1930's
Robert Price
Wayne Priest —1980
Bobby Rabold — 1995
David E. Rabold —1977
William Rabold, Jr. — 2008
Ron Raby — 2009
Kirby Ramsey — 1988
Dr. Gary Ransdell
Robbie Rather
W.E. Ray —1949
Sally Ray — 2000
Jeanette Rayles — 1994
W.H. Raymond — 1920's
Alan Read — 1991
Pete Reed
Jeffrey Reed —2003
Garland Reeves — 1952
Mike Reuter —1994
Brett Reynolds — 2007
Mike Reynolds — 1984
Charles H. Reynolds — 1970
Jody Richards — 1984
William H. Richeson — 1920's
John W. Ridley — 1977
Dr. E.R. Riggs — 1920's
Col. J.A. Robinson
John B. Rodes — 1936
Joel Rodgers — 1971
Hugh David Roe — 1999
William L. Roemer — 1937
Dr. Ed B. Rose — 1920 (charter)
Norman Ross
Norbert A. Rubano — 1970
Dr. Nelson Rue, Jr. — 1966
Marvin Russell — 1963
Clem W. Russell — 1942
Dr. B.S. Rutherford
H.S. Sanburn
Dixie Satterfield — 1987
John Scarborough — 1962
George Schenk
William E. Schiller
Major W.H. Schmid— 1930's
Paul Schnaes — 1985

Bob Schulten — 1983
Jim Scott
Dr. Barry Sears — 1988
Gale R. Seckel
Joe Secondine — 1996
James D. Shanahan — 1972
W.V. Shell
Ron Shrewsbury — 1963
Gen. W.L. Sibert — 1921
George Sikes
Glen E. Sikes
Charles T. Simmons
Kevin Simpson — 2002
Alice Simpson — 2009
Dr. David Simpson
Jim Skaggs — 1994
Ken Smart — 1995
Gordon Smith — 1940
Herbert Jones Smith — 1950
L.T. Smith — 1932
Robert Smith
Charles H. Smith
Raland Smith — 1920's
Ben Smith — 1988
Charles (Chuck) Smith —1969
Charles D. Smith — 2003
Janet Smith — 2003
David Smith — 1988
Gilbert Smith — 1958
Eddie Smith — 1990
Ryan Smith — 2008
Stephen Page Smith — 1976
Herb Smith, Jr. — 1979
David L. Sneed — 1951
Robert Soncrant —1989
David Sparks — 2002
Col. Robert Spiller — 1976
Fred Spires — 1939
Harold Stahl — 1969
Dr. Henry L. Stephens — 1940
Charles M. Stewart — 1948
Wallace Stewart
Cheryl Kirby Stokes — 2005
E.B. Stout — 1920 (charter)
Wes Strader — 1969

Clarence Strode
Harold Watson Sublett — 1920 (charter)
William C. Sumpter — 1921
Dr. Ward C. Sumpter — 1947
Rev. Howard Surface — 1960
Sharon Tabor — 2009
Clifford Talbert
Fred Tanner — 1975
John Tapscott — 1978
Joe W. Taylor — 1981
Ray Taylor — 1921
Sam Terry
Richard Thalacker — 1969
Jess B. Thomas
Jack Thomas — 1995
Linda Thomas — 1992
James R. Thompson — 1946
Steve Thornton —1985
James L. Thurber
Ed Tival — 1979
Dr. L.O. Toomey — 1953
Tony Torres — 1973
Robert (Bob) Toth — 1979
Lee Truman — 1964
Rev. Fred Turner
John E. Tyler — 1920's
Oscar Uhl — 1937
Leroy Underwood — 1974
Tom Updike — 1968
M.A. Vaughn — 1967
Alan Vilines — 2005
Mike Voyles — 1991
John Wade — 2008
Tony Walker — 1991
Kenneth R. (Kenny) Wallace — 1972
Mark Wallace — 1967
Bailey Walton — 1991
L.J. Waltz
Ron Ward — 1988
S.K. Warrener — 1920 (charter)
E.H. Warrener
J.H. Webb — 1950
Kenneth Webb —2006
Robert E. Weber — 1978
Paul Wedge

Jim Weisz — 1992
Ed Weldon — 1979
Jerry Wells — 2001
Donald Wendt — 1972
Walter Whitaker
Joe P. Wilk — 1958
Bruce Wilkerson —2008
Alvin Willendolf
Don L. Williams — 1970's
J. Mot Williams — 1920 (charter)
Dr. Jerome O. Williams
Rick Williams — 1998
Perry T. Williams
Robert Douglas Willock — 1934
Roland D. Willock — 1971
Dr. James O. Willoughby — 1960
Sterling Willoughby, Jr. — 1966
Harold E. Wills — 1970
Thomas M. Wilson — 1920's
Rick Wilson — 1999
Ron Wilson — 2001
Steve A. Wilson — 1990
Theo Withers
Mark Woodward — 1991
Ray Woosley — 1972
Jerry Wooten — 1996
William E. Wortham — 1963
Joan Wulff — 2008
Thomas L. Yelton — 1974
Dan Zoller — 2001

www.ingramcontent.com/pod-product-compliance
Lightning Source LLC
Chambersburg PA
CBHW071450040426
42444CB00008B/1283